Unlocking the Text

D0367968

Unlocking the Text

Fundamental Issues in Literary Theory

Jeremy Hawthorn

Professor of Modern British Literature,
University of Trondheim, Norway

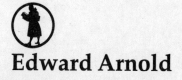

Edward Arnold

© Jeremy Hawthorn 1987

First published in Great Britain 1987 by
Edward Arnold (Publishers) Ltd, 41 Bedford Square, London WC1B 3DQ

Edward Arnold (Australia) Pty Ltd, 80 Waverley Road, Caulfield East,
  Victoria 3145, Australia

Edward Arnold, 3 East Read Street, Baltimore, Maryland 21202, USA

British Library Cataloguing in Publication Data
Hawthorn, Jeremy
  Unlocking the text: fundamental issues
  in literary theory.
  1. Literature——Philosophy
  I. Title
  801   PN45

Hum
PN
45
H38
1987

ISBN 0 7131 6427 1

All rights reserved. No part of this publication may be reproduced, stored in
a retrieval system, or transmitted in any form or by any means, electronic,
photocopying, recording or otherwise, without the prior permission of
Edward Arnold (Publishers) Ltd.

ROBERT MANNING
STROZIER LIBRARY

SEP 15 1988

Tallahassee, Florida

Text set in Linotron Palatino
by Northern Phototypesetting Co, Bolton
Made and printed in Great Britain by
Richard Clay Ltd, Bungay, Suffolk

Contents

Acknowledgements

The author and publishers would like to thank Roy Fisher and *Stand* Magazine for permission to quote the lines from 'One world' quoted on p. 114.

Preface

My excuse for producing yet another textbook on literary theory is that this one is concerned not with theorists and schools but with the essential problems these theorists and schools have attempted to tackle. There are some excellent textbooks available which provide detailed accounts of critics from Sidney to Barthes, or schools from the New Critics to the Deconstructionists. My experience as a teacher is that students at an early stage in the study of literature who are beginning to concern themselves with issues of literary theory are not always helped by syllabuses on literary theory which give them a large mass of descriptive material about critics and critical schools which has to be learned for an examination. Such a syllabus too quickly becomes just one more study area rather than the basis for study which informs all parts of a literature course. It *is* important to know about the history of literary criticism, about the theories, methods and approaches of influential critics and about the important groupings and movements in literary criticism. But first of all the student needs to know why such things are worth studying, and how they feed in to the study of literature.

This book, therefore, is designed to be used as an introduction to the scope of literary theory. It can profitably be used alongside a textbook giving more specific attention to individual critics and critical movements, but this is not essential. What is essential is that the student recognize that this is not a study apart; it is a study of the problems that are inevitably thrown up by the reading and discussion of literature.

When I started planning the book, I decided to try to write a book that made no reference to individual critics or theorists, that contained nothing of any originality, no personal opinions of my own, and that raised questions without suggesting answers. I soon found that to go this far would not be helpful to readers; certain problems are so bound up with the writings of particular critics that mention of their work and views is natural and helpful when discussing the problems. Moreover, even one's choice of problems suggests one's own priorities, and to offer no opinions of my own would have been artificial and – I venture to suggest – might have made the book too boring. But my original aims should suggest how I see this book: a guide to what literary theorists have found it important to discuss and argue about, and why. I hope that students will be able to relate the issues I discuss to their own reading and study of literature, to see these matters not as the specialist concern of isolated academics, but as problems that literary study leads intelligent readers towards.

My choice of examples is not generally very original, as my aim has been for clarity of exposition rather than that of shedding new light on traditional problems. I have lifted some examples from my own first book, *Identity and Relationship* (London, Lawrence & Wishart, 1973), and I am grateful to the publisher for permission to do this. Not all of my other examples are from primary sources. This is because I have been more concerned to find clear expositions of particular points of view than accurate representations of what a given authority actually maintains. As I have stated, not all 'Saussurean' views can be defended in terms of what can safely be attributed to Saussure – nevertheless, these views are influential, and I have taken some of them as clear statements of positions I have found it useful to discuss.

A short book such as this inevitably leaves much out and also fails to do full justice to the complexity of some issues. I hope, nonetheless, that it will help students – especially those nervous of or sceptical about literary theory – to see the relevance the study of literary theory has to their reading of literary works, and perhaps to pursue the issues I raise further.

Jeremy Hawthorn
March, 1987

I

Introductory

(i) Literature

A sensible way to begin to book on literary theory, the reader might reasonably presume, would be by giving a succinct and workable definition of what literary theory is. Many writers on literary theory in practice start rather differently – by explaining that the provision of such a working definition is difficult or impossible. Although this is doubtless rather frustrating for the reader, it is worth exploring why the term 'literary theory' is itself problematic, for such an explanation does have the virtue that it introduces many themes and issues central to literary theoretical debate. Why should it be that a term in such common use should present problems of definition?

To begin with, the term 'literature' is itself far from unproblematic. Asked by James Boswell, 'What is poetry?' Samuel Johnson replied, 'Why, Sir, it is much easier to say what it is not.' A number of recent commentators have suggested that such definition is difficult because terms like 'literature' or 'poetry' are open rather than closed, and that their meaning varies from age to age and culture to culture – and even within cultures.

Continuing his reply to Boswell, Johnson commented that, 'We all *know* what light is; but it is not easy to *tell* what it is.' In like manner it can be stated that we all know what poetry, or literature is, and that trying to define what 'we all know' is a time-wasting activity. The problem is that what 'we all know' turns out, on closer investigation, very often to involve an assumed rather than an actual agreement. This can be demonstrated both historically and in terms of our own contemporary attitudes. When English Literature developed as a university subject in Britain in the late nineteenth and early twentieth century, for example, the common assumption was that this would involve the study of poetry and drama rather than of the novel. It was also very often assumed that it would not include recent writing, and well into the 1960s certain British university departments of English were notorious for concluding their chronological coverage of English literature with late-nineteenth-century works.

If you look up the term 'literature' in the Oxford English Dictionary, you will find the following definition:

> Literary production as a whole; the body of writings produced in a particular country or period, or in the world in general. Now also in a more restricted sense, applied to writing which has claim to consideration on the ground of beauty of form or emotional effect.

Clear from this limited definition is the fact that in English there has been, historically, a narrowing down of the accepted meaning of the term 'literature'; from applying to 'the body of writings produced in a particular country or period', the scope of the term has suffered a diminution such that it now denotes a particular sort of writing, that possessed of 'a beauty of form' or that which is productive of a certain 'emotional effect'. The implications of this historical narrowing-down of the meaning of the term 'literature' will be looked at in more detail in due course; for the time being we can note that even the narrowed-down definition is by no means uncontroversial. Are there not things for which we look in order to decide whether we are reading 'literature' other than beauty of form and emotional effect? We can think of Brecht's desire to get his audiences to react intellectually rather than emotionally to his plays,[1] or of Wilfred Owen's *Preface* to his poems in which he states that,

> Above all I am not concerned with Poetry.
> My subject is War, and the pity of War.
> The Poetry is in the pity.[2]

Should Owen's implicit rejection of concern with 'beauty of form' and Brecht's of 'emotional effect' lead us to assume (if we agree that their works are as they describe them) that neither writer is a producer of literature?

A range of theorists have attempted to offer alternative definitions of literature which accord with what 'we all know', definitions based upon 'the language of literature', on literature's fictionality, or on some alternative view of its aesthetic appeal. But no such alternative definition has been found universally acceptable, and it would seem that 'literature' is a term which eludes watertight definition. Again, I will go into more detailed discussion of the implications that this fact has later on in the book; for the time being it is important that we are on our guard against too careless a use of the term 'literature'. We should remember not only that what is a work of literature to one person many fail to qualify as such to someone else, but also that

---

[1] See for example the essay, 'Theatre for Pleasure or Theatre for Instruction'.

[2] C. Day Lewis (ed.), *The Collected Poems of Wilfred Owen*, London, Chatto, 1963, p.31.

generalizations about literature may be only partially justified, may apply to some literary works and not to others.

One other point is worth making at this stage. The dictionary definition of literature quoted mentioned 'writings', and the etymology of the word 'literature' has a clear connection to writing. But in normal usage today 'literature' often has a rather wider scope, including oral productions and performance works. The way we divide the world up linguistically is often much more inflexible than might be desired; language often changes a continuum into a set of discrete stages or steps. In the pages to come I will try to indicate ways in which some of the problems about which I am talking can be illuminated by setting written literature alongside oral productions and the performing arts.

The narrowing-down of the scope of the term 'literature' during the past century or so has involved a shift from predominantly *descriptive* to *descriptive/evaluative* meanings. To refer to a work as a literary work today is to suggest something about its value. In his book *The Scholar-Critic* F. W. Bateson attempts to distinguish between 'literature', 'would-be literature', 'sub-literature', and 'non-literature'. He comments that

> Whatever literature is, it is not the poem or novel that is unreadable because of its total incompetence (would-be literature). Nor is it the pot-boiling journalism, whoever the author was, that is only potentially more than mere entertainment (sub-literature). Nor finally is it the use of language, in print or in speech, that is wholly trivial . . . or strictly utilitarian (non-literature).[3]

His three unsuccessful contenders to the condition of 'literature' Bateson argues, are 'subordinate verbal artifacts' which 'differ *toto caelo* from the *literary artifact* (in its various forms), if only because great literature represents by general agreement one of the pinnacles of human civilization.'

It is interesting that Bateson's argument here displays a not uncommon slippage; trying to talk about what *literature* is or is not, he very soon slips in to talking about *great literature* – as if it were unsatisfactory merely to talk of (by implication 'un-great') literature. More recently the theorist Stein Haugom Olsen makes it clear that for him the terms 'literature' and 'detective stories' are mutually exclusive.[4] It is apparent that for both Bateson and Olsen the term 'literature' is necessarily in part (or perhaps even in essence) an honorific one.

If we are to study literary theory then we need to remember that

[3] F. W. Bateson, *The Scholar-Critic*, London, Routledge, 1972, p.62.
[4] Stein Haugom Olsen, *The Structure of Literary Understanding*, Cambridge UP, pp.211–12.

what seem to be theoretical disagreements may turn out on closer inspection to involve differences of definition, disagreements about what 'literature' actually is. What is potentially very confusing is that often our implicit value-judgements alter without our being too conscious of the fact, without our realizing that the same terms and vocabulary can conceal shifting meanings. My impression is, for example, that by no means all readers and critics today would accept it as unproblematic to assume that 'literature' and 'detective fiction' were necessarily mutually exclusive. I recall a discussion in 1967 about the introduction of Film Studies as a university subject. One participant was guardedly enthusiastic about such a prospect, but noted that he took it for granted that by 'film' we were not including such things as the Western. Again, what 'we all know' today was apparently not known by certain people twenty years ago.

In recent years discussions concerning 'the canon' have high-lighted some of these problems. This term is of ecclesiastical origin: the canonical books were those accepted by the Church as part of the Bible. By extension, in literary studies 'the canon' came to designate those literary works accepted by university departments of literature as worthy of serious academic study – or, in some interpretations those works which merited the description 'literature'. Note, incidentally, that a canon implies a Church, an *institution* which makes selective and evaluative judgements. The canon in literary studies was not established by common readers, but by university academics, and very often a consciousness or unconsciousness of canonical distinctions can be seen to distinguish academic from non-academic readers.

It should be noted too that inclusion in the canon was normally argued in *de facto* terms: if most university departments of literature agreed that certain works merited serious study, then these works were, *ipso facto*, canonical. Subsequent explanations of the merit of these works might be ventured, but no abstract definition of what qualified a work for canonization could normally be found. One might be able to justify why Jane Austen's novels were canonical and Agatha Christie's were not, but as to *whether* these works were or were not on the canon there was no dispute: one could check the syllabuses in university departments of literature.

Now although this apparent unity about the canon was never complete (think, for instance, of F. R. Leavis's dismissal of the work of Laurence Sterne and Henry Fielding), it is certainly true that during the present century there have been long periods of relative agreement about what 'serious literature' or 'great literature' are, and by which works these categories are represented. But in more recent years the opening up of college and university literature syllabuses to popular literature (often directly or indirectly as a

result of the influence of Media Studies), and also with the development of campaigns for 'alternative' or 'lost' traditions – women
writers, working-class writers, writers from colonial backgrounds or
submerged groups – fierce argument about what is or is not worthy
of serious academic study 'as literature' has broken out. Such argument has perhaps revealed that beneath the seemingly monolithic
term 'literature' at different times and places is to be found a wide
variety of works, read, studied and enjoyed in a range of varying
ways.

'Read and studied' is a revealing phrase. 'Literature' today is
inescapably connected with education, both at school, college and
university level. One might cynically suggest that whereas people
read books, students study literature. The narrowing-down of the
meaning of the term 'literature' is intimately related to the growing
stress placed on a literary *education* by European and North
American societies.

Literary criticism is of course older than this development – much
older – but it is important to remember that what we refer to as
literary criticism may not have been described as such by the critic's
contemporaries. The Oxford English Dictionary, dating from the
early years of the present century, involves reference to a 'Literary
Man' and to a 'Critic' but not to a 'Literary Critic' – more evidence of
that narrowing down of the meaning of 'literature' and cognate
terms during the present century. We can surmise that the concept
of 'literature', and views of what criticizing literature involved, were
more open in the past than they are today, less seen in specialist or
quasi-technical ways than has been customary in the present
century. As I have suggested, there is little doubt that the increasing
association of literary studies with formal – and especially higher –
education is connected with such changes.

It is as well to bring this issue out into the open at this stage of this
book, for in one way or another it haunts literary theory and critical
theory. A general problem in all knowledge concerns the extent to
which our observations disturb, destroy or create what it is that we
are studying. With literature and criticism this problem is particularly acute: their study today is inescapably centred in academic
departments of literature, but these same departments are influential in defining what we see as literature, how it is to be critically
studied, and even (to a more limited extent) how it is to be written. Is
literary criticism then an activity that has been created by the
academy and has little or no relationship with the manner in which
'ordinary' (or 'common') readers read?

An adequate response to this question has to be more sophisticated than a simple 'yes' or 'no'. To start with, it needs to be pointed
out that there can be few – perhaps no – 'ordinary readers' whose

reading habits have not been at least partly formed through education. This has always been true in a general sense: someone always has to teach us to read. But in the present century the forming of reading habits has become more and more intimately linked with the educational *system*. Not only do most of us start reading literature at school, but our teachers have been trained in colleges and universities.

Nonetheless the ghost of the 'common reader' haunts literary theory – and rightly so, for it is central to questions about what literary criticism is. If the concept of 'literature' eludes watertight definition, we meet with further complications when we ask what it is that literary criticism actually studies or concerns itself with, what its object is. Does the literary critic typically study the work, the work in relation to its author, its time, or to other works, the reader's (or a reader's) response to or appreciation of the work, the meaning of the work (variously defined), or the significance and implications of the work (again as variously defined)? (For the time being I leave aside the complex question of the relationship between *text* and *work*, to which I shall return.)

If all this seems complicated enough, it is not hard to show that it is a considerable simplification of a more complex actuality. It is often assumed, for instance, that whereas literature is independent of literary criticism, literary criticism is parasitic on literature. But is literature independent of literary criticism? Are not our readerly expectations, or reading skills, or very view of what literature is, formed at least in part by literary criticism – particularly through its association with education? Would the novels and poems that are being written today have been written had no literary criticism been written? Moreover, when we come to trying to distinguish between 'reading', 'response', and 'criticism', then we soon realize that the three words – so conveniently discrete and separate – denote activities that cannot easily be distinguished one from another in any absolute sense.

These are all problems to which I will return. In the mean time I would like to suggest that it may be helpful, initially, to 'explode' literature into a number of more manageable components, to move, in short, from 'literature' to 'the literary process'. We can depict this process in a very simple form diagrammatically.

Like all such models this one has to be used with care if we wish to avoid being – in the words of George Eliot – ensnared by our metaphors. It is, for instance, potentially misleading to separate 'literary context' from 'socio-historical context', as the former is actually an aspect of the latter and inseparable from it. We can also posit that both the author and the literary and socio-historical contexts are in a sense 'in' the text as well as standing outside and apart

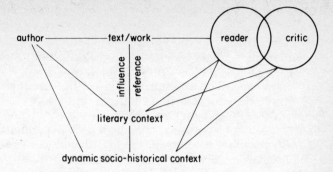

from it. As I shall point out later on in the book, it is also much less problematic to refer to 'the author' than to 'the reader'; most literary works have single authors and many readers, and this fact brings many attendant problems in its wake. Moreover, 'the reader' may read the same work many times.

For all this, the diagram has the virtue that it takes our attention away from literature as a 'thing', the text as an object demanding attention, and instead encourages us to consider 'literature' in terms of a set of shifting relationships which are never stable but which are all temporally mobile even if incorporated in and mediated through a relatively stable written text.

This is not to say that such a shift of emphasis is uncontroversial. It is clear that *some* theorists have believed that these relationships in some way or another actually create the work; take the following comment from M. M. Bakhtin:

> In the completely real-life time-space where the work resonates, where we find the inscription or the book, we find as well a real person – one who originates spoken speech as well as the inscription and the book – and real people who are hearing and reading the text. Of course these real people, the authors and the listeners and readers, may be (and often are) located in differing time-spaces, sometimes separated from each other by centuries and by great spatial distances, but nevertheless they are all located in a real, unitary and as yet incomplete historical world set off by a sharp and categorical boundary from the *represented* world in the text. Therefore we may call this world the world that *creates* the text, for all its aspects . . . participate equally in the creation of the represented world in the text.
>
> . . .
>
> However forcefully the real and the represented world resist fusion, however immutable the presence of that categorical boundary line between them, they are nevertheless indissolubly tied up with each other and find themselves in continual mutual interaction; uninterrupted exchange goes on between them, similar to the uninterrupted

exchange of matter between living organisms and the environment that
surrounds them. As long as the organism lives, it resists a fusion with the
environment, but if it is torn out of its environment, it dies.[5]

Bakhtin's statement is a classic example of a dialectical or relational
view of literature, a view that assumes that literature is only under-
standable in the context of an appreciation of the dynamic relationships between the various aspects of the literary process.

Against such a view can be set the alternative view that literature
can, should, and in some versions, must be seen independently of
such relationships, in terms of itself. We find this view in various
versions of Formalism, amongst which I would include certain
Structuralist formulations. David Robey, for example, writing about
'Modern Linguistics and the Language of Literature', expounds the
following version of what has been claimed to be a 'Saussurean'
view of literature:

> . . . if the literary text is seen as a sign or set of signs in the Saussurean
> sense, then its meaning or content must be the product of a structure of
> relationships or differences whose connection with the 'real' world is
> purely arbitrary.[6]

On the one hand we have a view of literature that sees it in perpetual
and necessary symbiotic exchange with the real world; on the other
hand we have a view of literature with a purely arbitrary (and
presumably, therefore, unilluminating) connection with a world
that is of so little substance that it can only be referred to as 'real'
rather than as real. (This last smacks somewhat of overkill: if the
world is not real then one needs hardly waste time discussing
whether or not it is in a necessary or defining relationship with the
literary text.) It is probably clear from my presentation of these
views that my own sympathy lies with the former rather than the
latter view; my own feeling is that rather than starting the investigation of literature by attempting to define literature, it makes better
sense to work towards an understanding of the conditions necessary for the existence of literature – literature's 'productive relations'. Unlike many theorists, then, I do not start from what can be
termed an 'essentialist' conception of literature, but from a more
pragmatic and dialectical view. This view has something in common
with what has been termed the institutional view of literature – that
is, an approach to the understanding of literature that looks not for
an essential quality in the 'thing' (the literary work) itself, but in the

[5] M. M. Bakhtin, *The Dialogic Imagination*, ed. Michael Holquist; trans. Caryl Emerson
and Michael Holquist, Austin, U. of Texas Press, 1981, pp.253, 254.
[6] David Robey, 'Modern Linguistics and the Language of Literature', in Ann Jefferson and David Robey (eds.), *Modern Literary Theory*, London, Batsford, 1982, p.46.

system of assumptions, customs and rules which gives the literary work meaning and upon which the writer in some sense depends. In spite of this similarity I am critical of many actual examples of institutional theories of literature because they seem to me to underestimate the degree of disagreement and development in the 'institution' of literature. Comparisons between this institution and the monetary system or the rules of chess have the virtue of exposing the shortcomings of essentialist approaches to literature, but it should be apparent that they involve comparisons with far more unified and stable rule-systems than can be found to operate with literary works.

The history of criticism – I would suggest – can be seen as the history of attempts to understand literature in terms of successive parts of the literary process, only rarely involving all of these parts in their dynamic interrelations. Literary criticism in this view is the history of a sequence of exclusions – excluding the author, the reader, the literary or socio-historical context – or the transformations of history as the text survives through a range of different historical situations.

But at this point perhaps we should proceed to some introductory comments concerning criticism.

(ii) Criticism

If there are problems in defining exactly what we mean by 'literature', there are no fewer when we turn to 'criticism'. In the following introductory comments I will start by outlining some general problems of definition and demarcation, and then proceed to more specific commentary upon different critical activities. 'Criticism,' we soon realize, is something of a blanket term, one which covers a wide range of different activities, and one which is impossible to separate off from unambiguously non-critical procedures in any totally satisfactory way. Take for example the question of the relationship between reading and criticizing. Are these discrete and easily separable activities, or does each in some way necessarily involve the other? Is criticism a *post facto* procedure, one which starts once reading has finished, or is an adequate reading itself critical in essence?

The answer to such a question, not very surprisingly, has to be that it all depends what one means by 'criticism' and 'reading'. Both are alarmingly elastic terms in current literary-critical usage, and need to be broken down into their component parts – or mapped on the terrain of their typical deployment – to clarify matters. Just as we approached a discussion of 'literature' by turning our attention to the components of the literary process, so too can 'criticism' be at least partially demystified by considering different critical activities.

Literary criticism, literary theory, critical theory

Let us begin, however, with the promised consideration of some general problems of definition and demarcation. First of all, let us consider three confusingly related terms: 'literary criticism', 'literary theory', 'critical theory'. Many readers may well feel that a simple way of drawing boundaries might be by saying that literary criticism is concerned with the practical criticism of particular texts, literary theory with the general knowledge of the nature of literature that can be abstracted from literary criticism, and critical theory with the study of literary criticism itself. And as a rule-of-thumb guide these suggested areas of concern are not unhelpful. Thus we can further distinguish literary theory from critical theory by saying that the latter is derived from and directed towards the practical criticism of particular literary texts, with 'practical criticism' denoting not the narrower 'close reading' associated with the critic I. A. Richards, but a wide range of activities including interpretation, analysis, contextualization, explication, and so on. (For further comment on these terms see below.) Literary theory, in contrast would involve a more general concern with the nature, rôle(s) and function(s) of literature, dealing not so much with what we do with literary works as critics, but with what they are and what their range of functions is.

Although such a neat set of definitions has much to recommend it, we have to contend with the fact that current usage tends to be a lot more untidy. 'Literary theory', for example, is often used as a wider, generic term to embrace both what we can call the aesthetics of literature and also the theory of literary criticism. 'Critical theory' is also a somewhat problematic term as it can indicate either an implicit set of beliefs informing a given piece of literary criticism, or it can denote a meta-critical level of theorizing concerned with what literary criticism is and what it does. And 'literary criticism' in practice is used to refer to a bewildering range of different activities, a summary of which I shall attempt to produce towards the end of this section.

Moreover, theory can be either descriptive or normative: it can either argue that 'this is how literary criticism proceeds', or 'this is how literary criticism *should be* conducted'.

The importance of realizing how flexible some of the terms we are dealing with actually are in normal use is well exemplified by the arguments of Steven Knapp and Walter Benn Michaels in their influential article 'Against Theory'. They produce a definition of 'theory' early on in the article, and this definition is arguably a rather narrow and tendentious one:

> By 'theory' we mean a special project in literary criticism: the attempt to govern interpretations of particular texts by appealing to an account of interpretation in general.[7]

They note that the term 'theory' is sometimes applied to literary subjects with no direct bearing on the interpretations of individual works, subjects such as narratology, stylistics, or prosody, but argue that these are essentially empirical in nature, and thus despite their generality, outside of the scope of their attack on theory.

But as I have already suggested, 'literary theory' is not necessarily associated with 'the attempt to govern interpretations of particular texts'; in some usages it denotes, rather, a general study of the nature of literature based upon abstraction from actual literary-critical practice. In this wider sense, for example, literary theorists would or could be interested in studying the nature of composition, investigating such matters as influence, inspiration, and the writer's sense of an audience. Now it would be wrong to suggest that such matters were necessarily irrelevant to the interpretation of individual literary texts (although many critics have argued that they are), but it is certainly the case that they can be investigated independent of any concern to govern interpretations of particular texts. Much the same could be said about a wide range of other activities which are sometimes included under the umbrella of literary theory, especially when 'literary theory' is used as a synonym or near-synonym for 'literary aesthetics'.

Again, 'critical theory' is a term that in practice covers a somewhat extended continuum from 'theoretical presuppositions implicit in certain literary-critical acts' to 'an attempt to govern interpretations of particular texts by appealing to an account of interpretation in general'. Knapp and Michaels do not distinguish between 'literary theory' and 'critical theory', and their discussion can be accused of setting up an Aunt Sally which then they proceed to knock down.

Critical method

'Critical method' is a term presenting rather fewer problems. The actual techniques used by a literary critic are related directly or indirectly to the theoretical presuppositions and assumptions which inform his or her criticism, although the critic may not be aware of this, and although a critic may deploy methods which are not logically compatible with his or her professed theoretical standpoint. (Thus, for example, the New Critics have been accused

[7] Steven Knapp and Walter Benn Michaels, 'Against Theory', repr. in W. J. T. Mitchell (ed.), *Against Theory: Literary Studies and the New Pragmatism*, London, U. of Chicago Press, 1985, p.11.

of bringing 'extrinsic' information to the analysis of poetry in a covert manner, whilst claiming that the critical use of such material was inadmissable.) Critics of very different theoretical persuasions may actually utilize similar or even identical critical techniques in their analysis of a given work of literature, such that from an extract taken from their criticism it may be hard or impossible to identify their theoretical presuppositions. This of course is one of the reasons why dialogue is possible between critics holding widely different theoretical beliefs, and why it is often instructive and rewarding to read the criticism of those with whom one is not in theoretical agreement.

I have used the word 'techniques' above, and it is useful to subdivide critical method into higher- and lower-level elements, which we can conveniently label 'methods' and 'techniques'. Thus when T. S. Eliot remarks that comparison and analysis are the chief tools of the critic we can assume that he is talking about techniques rather than methods, especially as he proceeds to distinguish comparison and analysis from interpretation, remarking that whereas the former 'need only the cadavers on the table; . . . interpretation is always producing parts of the body from its pockets, and fixing them in place.'[8] The comment is by no means completely clear in its implications, and it occurs in the context of an essay which regards the activity of interpretation with considerable suspicion, but nonetheless it suggests a contrast between a more mechanical, fact-based activity and one which is creative and which in some sense produces its own facts. Not surprisingly, a critic's theoretical persuasion is more likely to be revealed in his or her method than in his or her techniques.

Thus in very general terms we could give as examples of critical method a critic's attempt to understand or explicate a work in terms of its generic nature, or in terms of its relationship with its genesis, or in terms of the wider human problems with which it is concerned. Critical techniques would involve Eliot's comparison and analysis, but also the use of paraphrase, the tracing of themes in a novel or patterns of imagery in a poem, and so on. Clearly we are dealing with a continuum rather than a sharply distinguished pair of alternatives here; analysis very often involves reference to generic factors or to the writer's biography, and the tracing of patterns of imagery in a poem can also involve a discussion of the wider human problems with which the work is concerned.

Often, the more self-conscious a critic is about theoretical assumptions, the more he or she will attempt to assess methods and

[8] T. S. Eliot, 'The Function of Criticism', repr. in *Selected Essays*, London, Faber, repr. 1969, p.33.

techniques to see if they are fully compatible with these assumptions. Critics can be more or less pragmatic, and the more pragmatic the more a critic will assess methods and techniques in terms of their immediate results rather than in terms of their compatibility with a given set of theoretical assumptions. Moreover, critical disagreements normally assume a different form when they occur at the level of technique from when they occur at the more general level of method. There is a difference between saying that a critic is doing something badly, and saying that he or she should not be doing something at all. Take, for example, some of the classic debates between critics of Milton's 'Paradise Lost' in the decades immediately after the Second World War. In his book *Milton's God* William Empson makes it clear that many of these involve genuine disagreements about what a critic faced with a literary work from another culture should do:

> A curious trick has been played on modern readers here; they are told: 'Why, but of course you must read the poem taking for granted that Milton's God is good; not to do that would be absurdly unhistorical. Why, the first business of a literary critic is to sink his mind wholly into the mental world of the author, and in a case like this you must accept what they all thought way back in early times.' I think this literary doctrine is all nonsense anyhow; A critic ought to use his own moral judgement, for what it is worth, as well as to try to understand the author's, and that is the only way he can arrive at a 'total reaction.'[9]

The particular issue involved here I will consider further on in the book when I discuss the issue of the 'Suspension of Disbelief'; for the time being I would merely wish to draw attention to the fact that critical disagreements between critics may involve not only dispute about what is true, but about what is appropriate or relevant, and debates about critical method classically lead to the latter of these two alternatives.

Critical approach

The term 'critical approach' is less precise than 'critical method', but it is in such common use that some comment on it is appropriate. It normally covers both a critic's (implicit or explicit) theoretical assumptions and also his or her methods and techniques. The critical approach of a New Critic such as Cleanth Brooks, for example, involved both a set of assumptions concerning the secondary importance of such things as biographical information about the writer, information about the work's genesis, and so on, and also a set of familiar methods and techniques – starting with 'the words on

[9] William Empson, *Milton's God*, London, Chatto, revised ed. 1965, p.204.

the page', tracing patterns of imagery, discreet use of paraphrase, and so on.

Very often schools or types of criticism are referred to as 'approaches' – thus we find reference to 'the Marxist approach' or 'the Psychological approach' in many textbooks. We should remember that such labels can be used descriptively as well as proscriptively; 'the Marxist approach' is thus the way in which Marxist critics are claimed typically to have criticized literature, or alternatively, that form of literary criticism which merits the description 'Marxist'.

Reading

'Reading' is a topic that will be looked at in depth as part of a consideration of 'Reception' in section VI. It is worth engaging in some preliminary discussion of the term at this point however, as different writers refer to a wide range of different activities under its umbrella. It is true that the last couple of decades have witnessed a striking development (or revival) of interest in reading among literary critics, and that this may be part of the reason for the complexity of the term today, but if we look up the verb 'to read' in the Oxford English Dictionary we discover that this complexity already existed at the time the OED was compiled at the start of the present century. The dictionary gives us a surprisingly long list of alternative meanings, ranging from 'to make out the meaning of' through 'to inspect and interpret in thought (any signs which represent words or discourse)' and 'to look over or scan (something written, printed, etc.) with understanding of what is meant by the letters and signs', to figurative meanings involving a rather more general concept of the 'interpretation of signs and words'.

In summary, we can suggest that the central dictionary definitions, as well as distinguishing between the transitive and intransitive usages, and between silent and voiced reading, draw our attention to a distinction between reading as decoding (that is, the accurate establishment of verbal meaning), and reading as interpretation (that is, in very broad terms, the consideration of the significance and implications of that verbal meaning). It may well be that we are again concerned with a continuum rather than a neat and absolute divide here; after all, we cannot establish verbal meaning without some sense of implication and significance. Nonetheless, the distinction between these two senses of 'to read' is a useful and illuminating one. It should be clear that the distinction is not directed specifically or exclusively at either literature or literary criticism, as is apparent from the following quotation from Michael Stubbs's book *Language and Literacy:*

> There is . . . still no general agreement on what is meant by *reading* and *literacy* . . . Most collections of articles on reading contain papers with titles such as 'What is reading?', 'The nature of reading', or even 'Reading: is there such a thing?' . . . The basic debate has been between those who hold that reading means essentially the 'mechanics' of reading, that is, the ability to decode written words into spoken words; and those who maintain that reading essentially involves understanding.[10]

Stubbs's distinction here is not identical to the one I extracted from the dictionary definitions of 'reading'; if we put them together we actually get three relatively distinct meanings: (i) decoding written words into spoken words; (ii) establishing verbal meaning; (iii) moving to an understanding of the written text which involves a consideration of its significance and implications. Stubbs describes the third alternative as 'essentially a process related to the social uses to which writing is put', and gives an interesting practical example of what this may involve. He posits a situation in which a layman possessed of a complicated legal document rings up a solicitor, who considers what he hears read to him and explains the relevant passages to his client. Clearly the layman reads but does not fully understand what he reads: this is quite different from reading a book with complete understanding.

One of the reasons why 'reading' can be such a confusing term is that it covers such a range of varying activities. When we ask, therefore, what the relationship between reading and criticizing a literary work is, it is inevitable that the initial response must be, 'It depends what you mean by "reading".' Indeed, once we turn to the reading of complex literary texts then the problem of levels of understanding becomes much more pressing. When we say that we have read *Bleak House* we do not mean that we have unthinkingly and unreflectingly rendered the written text into spoken utterance. Nor do we mean that we have gone through the text as proof-readers are supposed to be able to do, concerning themselves only with so much of the text's verbal meaning as is necessary to determine whether or not it contains any misprints.

We say that one can become a more and more proficient reader of literature, and that the more accomplished one becomes the more complexities of meaning and significance one is responsive to. One way of expressing this is to say that one becomes a more competent reader of literature by studying and practising literary criticism – one becomes, in brief, able to *read critically*. This would suggest that the more skilled a literary critic one becomes, the more reading and criticizing converge. On the other hand, however, certain critical

[10]Michael Stubbs, *Language and Literacy*, London, Routledge, 1980, pp.4, 5.

activities (as we will shortly observe) are necessarily *post facto*, are activities which follow rather than accompany response and interpretation, the response and interpretation that form a more integrated aspect of intelligent reading.

We should always remember that the difficulty we have in defining and distinguishing some of the terms that I have introduced may stem from the complexity of the activities they are intended to isolate and describe. Let us imagine, for example, stopping in the middle of reading a complex and lengthy literary work. At this point one thinks about what has been read so far, one re-lives reading experiences – perhaps immersing oneself imaginatively in the life of the work, – and one allows one's imagination to play over what is likely to occur in the pages to come. Is this 'reading', 'responding', or 'criticizing'? One could defend referring to it by any one of these three terms.

Response

Having mentioned 'responding', some comments on the issue of literary response are in order at this point. 'Response' is a far less fashionable critical term today than it has been at times in the recent past. For many critics today it carries rather unscientific and self-indulgent connotations which are not in accord with the mood of the times. Nonetheless, it is a useful term, useful because it isolates an aspect of the literary process that is inadequately dealt with by other alternatives. Response, put simply, is what happens to us when and as a result of reading a work of literature. Discussion of response follows naturally on from discussion of reading, because it is arguable that response begins at that point on the reading continuum at which the reader moves from as it were *finding* to *using* the meaning of the words and sentences in the literary text. What is useful about the term 'response' is that it is unambiguously creative and personal, belonging to the reader rather than to the author, however much it may be based on appreciation of a text's verbal meaning. When an individual responds to our verbal or non-verbal behaviour, that response is necessarily *theirs* and not *ours*, even if we have called it forth. If we wish to talk of a part of the reading experience that is to be attributed to the reader and not the text or the author, therefore, 'response' is a useful term.

Some qualifications are in order, however. Firstly, that response normally denotes what happens during or soon after reading: the term implies a relatively immediate and unmediated reaction to the text. The critical theory about 'Paradise Lost' which comes into my mind ten years after having read the poem would not normally be referred to as a response to the work. Secondly, although I have said that a reader's response is his or hers rather than the text's or the author's, this does not mean that different readers cannot have very similar responses to the same text; in fact this is very often found to be the case. Critics make much of critical disagreements about texts, but in their writing they often (sometimes without admitting it) assume a set of common elements in readers' responses to the same text, especially when the readers concerned have much in common. (Literary responses are, in this respect, not unlike other sorts of response.)

In his Preface to the Second Edition of *Seven Types of Ambiguity*, William Empson uses the word 'reaction' to encompass much that I wish to describe as 'response', and he points out, usefully, that we can often 'react' without understanding what our reaction is composed of or caused by.

> Now I was frequently puzzled in considering my examples . . . I felt sure that the example was beautiful and that I had, broadly speaking, reacted to it correctly. But I did not at all know what had happened in this 'reaction'; I did not know why the example was beautiful. And it seemed to me that I was able in some cases partly to explain my feelings to myself by teasing out the meanings of the text.[11]

Empson goes on to argue that once teased out, the examples were often too complicated to be remembered together, just as in ordinary life we can often see our way out of a situation when it would be extremely hard to separate out all the elements of the judgement. In this view, analysing the text (or, to be precise, Empson says 'the meanings of the text') is a way in to understanding one's own reaction (or response) as reader.

Two points can be made about this view of response. Firstly, that *by implication*, Empson assumes that the reactions of competent readers are very similar, as they can all be traced back to the same elements in the text. And secondly, that even though a response may be unambiguously the reader's, it belongs by proxy to the author as well, if it can be explained and understood in terms of specific textual features. Not all critics have made such assumptions, and many have shied away from discussion of response precisely because they feel that response is so personal and idiosyncratic that critical discussion of it is vain. In their essay 'The Affective Fallacy' Monroe Beardsley and W. K. Wimsatt discuss 'affect' in these terms, and clearly assume that the affect of one text will vary from person to person and probably also from reading to reading.

[11] William Empson, Preface to the Second Edition of *Seven Types of Ambiguity*, Harmondsworth, Penguin, repr. 1965, p.x.

> The Affective Fallacy is a confusion between the poem and its *results* (what it *is* and what it *does*). . . . It begins by trying to derive the standard of criticism from the psychological effects of the poem and ends in impressionism and relativism.
>
> . . .
>
> The report of some readers . . . that a poem or story induces in them vivid images, intense feelings, or heightened consciousness, is neither anything which can be refuted nor anything which it is possible for the objective critic to take into account.[12]

Beardsley and Wimsatt's assumption that the affects of a single work are not constant from reader to reader is clearly at odds with Empson's confidence in his ability to work back to textual detail from a reaction isolated through introspection. The gap between the two critical positions is symptomatic of a number of problems thrown up by the central fact that part of what happens to a reader during the reading of a work is personal – even private and idiosyncratic – and part is shared to a greater or lesser extent with other readers.

Unfashionable though it may be, therefore, the issue of response is central to many fashionable disputes and disagreements.

I have said that 'response' normally denotes what happens during or soon after an actual reading. We can extend this point by stressing that what our terminology has to come to grips with is the fact that the inner processes and reactions engendered in an individual by a literary reading are continuing and developing. The literary work *works in* us and we *work on* it – both individually and collectively. There are some works of literature which I read over twenty years ago and to which I have not yet returned which are still generating fresh mental processes in me. Now our vocabulary suggests that the nature of such processes changes over time, that the sort of processes enjoyed during or soon after the reading of a work are different from those which develop some time after completion of a reading. The pragmatic distinction made by many critics between 'reading' (or 'response') and 'criticism' relates to this perceived distinction. It is as if we moved from a set of experiences 'within' the world of the work to viewing the work more from outside, more objectively. We are perhaps able progressively to distance ourselves from our own reading experiences or responses. We move from being mastered by the work to trying, on some level, to master it. Now there is clearly some truth in such a view, but we should beware of accepting it unreflectingly. As I have already suggested, we can read (and respond) critically, distancing ourselves from our own reading experiences. And we can sink back into

---

[12] W. K. Wimsatt and Monroe C. Beardsley, 'The Affective Fallacy', in *The Verbal Icon*, London, Methuen, 1970, pp.21, 32.

the world of the work – even years after we have put the book down for the last time. In summary, our relations with and reactions to a work during and after reading it are dynamic and volatile. The critic Douglas Hewitt, referring specifically to the novel, argues that we have not paid sufficient attention to what is 'probably the most basic of all the conflicts within fiction'

> that between the novel as object and the novel as process. A novel is both a created object to which we look back and an experience which we undergo . . . To say that a novel is a created object is, of course, a metaphorical way of putting it. What we actually grasp is a recollection of a temporal process, of a series of experiences, of responses to imagined situations, of progress from one point to another.[13]

We can say, then, that 'reading', 'responding' and 'criticizing' are terms which designate separable but also necessarily interconnected activities. It is useful to be able to distinguish what goes on in a reader's head while he or she is reading a work, from that reader's consideration of the work and his or her response subsequent to the reading experience. But it is important to realize once again that we are dealing with the two ends of a continuum rather than with two unproblematically separate processes.

If this seems disturbingly vague, it may be a relief to turn more directly to the activities of the critic, for these can be categorized with rather more precision. This is not to say that what criticism is is unproblematic, for if as has been suggested the whole relationship between reading and criticism is complex then this can hardly be the case. And many of the problems and issues with which I will deal in the pages to come make of criticism a site for disagreements rather than a peaceful abode of agreed procedures. It is, however, possible to separate out a number of discrete critical *activities* and to comment upon these individually in an introductory manner. By so doing one can both introduce certain key issues which will be dealt with in more detail in subsequent chapters, and also clarify the meaning and application of certain key critical terms. The following comments, therefore, should be looked upon as attempts to introduce various problems, rather than as pronouncements intended to stifle debate. It is important that we remember that critics do a range of different things, and that such different activities involve widely varying problems. In his book *Philosophy and the Novel* Peter Jones quotes a remark from the pianist Alfred Brendel, who declared that he considered his rôle as a performer to embrace three aspects:

---

[13] Douglas Hewitt, *The Approach to Fiction*, London, Longman, 1972, p.188.

As a museum clerk he needed to establish the text; as a solicitor he engaged in the moral activity of doing the best he could for his client; as a midwife he assisted at the birth of a new creation, even though he had done similar things before.[14]

Now although Brendel is talking of performance, his remarks, as Peter Jones points out, are relevant to the discussion of interpretation, and thus to the rôle of the critic.

Critical activities

1 Scholarship

In current usage the activity of scholarship is normally considered distinguishable from that of criticism, although, confusingly, as the term 'scholar' has become less widely used it has become accepted that it is usually the critic who engages in scholarly work. Scholarship and criticism are, nevertheless, very closely allied with one another, and in the opinion of many neither can be carried on in total independence from the other (an opinion reflected in F. W. Bateson's term 'scholar-critic'). Scholarship is conventionally understood to imply the *establishment* of facts rather than their interpretation. A scholar seeks to establish such things as the precise text by which an author wished his or her work to be represented (a far more problematic matter than may at first appear to be the case), or facts relating to a work's publication, an author's life, experiences, expressed beliefs and intentions, or contextual information relating to the author's contemporaries, society, and so on.

Dealing with 'facts' sounds unproblematic in a theoretical sense, although clearly involving considerable (even insuperable) practical problems. In actuality 'facts' and interpretative opinions turn out to be often well-nigh indistinguishable: establishing a text, for example, often involves the interpretation of ambiguous or incomplete information, and the *sort* of interpretation concerned is very often of a literary–critical variety. Scholarship is very often intertwined with interpretative activities through the investigation of a work's cultural and historical contexts. Could a writer be referring to a particular event or belief in a given work? Is it technically possible that work 'A' by writer 'B' could have been read by writer 'C' and thus have served as an influence on work 'D'? Although such inquiry is obviously associated with the establishment of objective facts, the felt need to pursue such inquiries proceeds from the desire to solve interpretative problems – or it should do. (The establishment of 'facts' independent of any possible

---

[14] Peter Jones, *Philosophy and the Novel*, Oxford, Clarendon Press, 1975, p.194.

interpretative need has on occasion given scholarship a bad name –
witness Yeats's poem 'The Scholars'.)

In his book *The Scholar-Critic* F. W. Bateson argued that criticism
and scholarship were 'complementary, both indispensable, both
equally honourable aspects of a single discipline.'[15] It is as pointless to
engender successive interpretations in blithe ignorance of textual or
contexual actuality as it is to amass facts independent of any interpretative need.

At this juncture it is perhaps worth saying a few words about the
term 'research'. This is complicated by its having become part of the
vocabulary of academic management in higher education: colleges
and universities have 'research budgets', 'research leave', and so
on. Literary critics who are academics thus find themselves under
institutional pressure to describe much of what they do as literary
critics as 'research', even though, strictly speaking, research
involves (in the words of the dictionary), an 'endeavour to find out
new facts'. It is clear that the influence of the pure and applied
sciences is apparent in this usage, and it has led to some valorizing
of scholarship at the expense of criticism in contexts where literary
critics have had to demonstrate the respectability of their profession
to colleagues in other disciplines.

In practice, most academic disciplines involve both a need to
establish facts and a requirement to engage in critical and interpretative activity, and literary criticism is probably less unique in this
respect than is sometimes assumed. But because of the institutional
pressures I have mentioned above, we can often detect a sort of
'backlash' effect, whereby literary critics dismiss or denigrate
scholarship as a mechanical activity, on a lower level of importance
from what is seen as criticism proper. As I have already indicated, I
find this attitude to be mistaken.

2 Explication

In English, 'explication' normally denotes the uncovering of what
we may refer to as a literary work's 'primary meaning', as distinct
from those deeper levels of meaning and significance produced by
interpretation. This distinction is by no means unproblematic, as we
will see below when we look at terms such as 'interpretation' and
'meaning' more closely. It is obviously not the case that all literary
works have simple, unproblematic literal meanings, on which more
complex interpretations can be based. The 'simple meaning' of a
word in a poem may only be determinable as a result of detailed
analytical and interpretative activity. To say what the 'primary
meaning' of the twice-used word 'ye' is in the final line of Keats's

---

[15] Bateson, p.vii.

'Ode on a Grecian Urn', one needs to engage not just in syntactical and grammatical analysis, but in literary–critical interpretation. But yet having said this, and having admitted that the distinction between 'primary meaning' and 'interpretation' is a highly problematic one, nevertheless one wants to be able to have a term which describes the activity of establishing the meaning of the words and sentences in a literary work at a relatively mechanical level.

A further complication here is that the French term *explication de texte* denotes a form of textual study and analysis which includes both the establishment of a text's primary meaning along with what in English we would refer to as interpretative activities – and this extended meaning has influenced the way in which the word 'explication' is used in English. In practice, then, this term can be used in rather different ways, although it generally has a narrower and more technical/formal range of meanings than has the term 'interpretation'. Very often explication will concentrate upon the elucidation of textual cruces – baffling words in or sections of literary works which seem not to make sense. Here the relationship between explication, scholarship, and interpretation is very close: and all three activities can be detected in the process whereby we attempt to resolve problems of disputed or puzzling readings.

3 Interpretation

With interpretation we move to one of the most problematic and disputed terms in literary–theoretical debate. Put simply, we can say that a central dispute revolves around the question as to whether interpretation is an activity dedicated to the uncovering of authorial meaning, or whether interpretation is in some sense creative, in some sense involves the production of something additional to authorial meaning. (I should point out that the phrase 'authorial meaning' is itself by no means unproblematic, and some of the issues raised by its use will be considered below.)

We can find a comparable variation of the meaning of 'interpretation' outside of the realms of literary criticism and critical theory. The OED includes among its definitions of 'interpret' the following: 'to expound the meaning of', 'to elucidate', 'to explain', 'to translate' (obsolete apart from the cognate noun 'interpreter'), and 'In recent use: to give one's own interpretation of (a musical composition, a landscape, etc.)'.

Summarizing the range of definitions given here, we can make a broad distinction between interpretation as *a process of getting at, revealing, or communicating a pre-existing meaning*, and interpretation as *a process of creating something new and personal to the interpreter as an extension of a pre-existing text*. In brief – the interpreter as elucidator/ translator and the interpreter as creative performer or producer; the interpreter as midwife and the interpreter as parent. On the one hand the simultaneous translator at the United Nations whose job it is to transpose someone else's words into another language with (ideally) no addition or subtraction of meaning; on the other hand the virtuoso interpreter of a violin concerto or of *Hamlet* who creates something new, unique, and valuable out of a pre-existing score or text.

Much of the debate between literary critics and critical theorists concerning interpretation can be characterized as a debate between those committed to these two different views of interpretation. This might suggest that we are dealing with what is fundamentally a terminological dispute, but this is not the case. It is true that terminological issues enter into the matter: thus the American theorist E. D. Hirsch has suggested a distinction between 'meaning' and 'significance', with the former seen as the end of interpretation and the latter the result of a different process. For Hirsch, therefore, the interpreter is midwife rather than parent, dedicated to the uncovering of authorial meaning. As he puts it

> *Meaning* is that which is represented by a text; it is what the author meant by his use of a particular sign sequence; it is what the signs represent. *Significance*, on the other hand, names a relationship between that meaning and a person, or a conception, or a situation, or indeed anything imaginable.[16]

Such a distinction, if accepted, might conceivably allow us to distinguish between interpretation and, say, discussion of significance (or, possibly, appreciation). Those theorists who persisted in seeing the interpreter to be responsible for discussing a work's significance would be falling foul of Hirsch's terminological rules, but not necessarily suggesting a form of activity that was – according to Hirsch – necessarily illegitimate. But the central debate to which I have alluded involves more than such terminological issues.

In particular, at issue have been the *authority* of the author or of the text, and the *freedom* of the interpreter to do what he or she likes with a text: in short, the extent to which an interpreter of a text is constrained in certain ways as to the interpretation which can be produced and the extent to which he or she is free to generate interpretations. We may again speak of a continuum: at one end of this the interpreter is like a taxi-driver, whose job it is to find the address determined by the passenger/author. At the other end of the continuum the interpreter's relationship with the author and

---

[16] E. D. Hirsch Jnr., *Validity in Interpretation*, London, Yale UP, 1976, p.8. An excellent critique of the view that it is helpful to talk of a literary work's 'meaning' can be found in Stein Haugom Olsen, 'The Meaning of a Literary Work', *New Literary History* XIV, 1982–1983, pp.13–32.

with the text is more like that of driver to car-manufacturer: once the car has been bought the driver can drive it anywhere he or she wants.

For Hirsch the interpreter is clearly elucidator/translator rather than creative performer, and his arguments have carried much weight in recent years. They have not gone unchallenged however, and they are in stark contrast to other very influential opinions – opinions which are by no means limited to Deconstructionists or Structuralists. A classic statement advocating interpretative freedom comes from T. S. Eliot's 'The Frontiers of Criticism':

> The first danger is that of assuming that there must be just one interpretation of the poem as a whole, that must be right. There will be details of explanation, especially with poems written in another age than our own, matters of fact, historical allusions, the meaning of a certain word at a certain date, which can be established, and the teacher can see that his pupils get these right. But as for the meaning of the poem as a whole, it is not exhausted by an explanation, for the meaning is what the poem means to different sensitive readers. The second danger . . . is that of assuming that the interpretation of a poem, if valid, is necessarily an account of what the author consciously or unconsciously was trying to do.[17]

It is not just a different terminology that separates Eliot from Hirsch (as Hirsch recognizes); Eliot is prepared to privilege or authenticate interpretations (by which he means attributions of meaning) which are purely personal and which are not and could not have been sanctioned by the author.

Another Eliot – George – included the wry comment that 'Signs are small measurable things, but interpretations are illimitable' in the third chapter of her novel *Middlemarch*, a comment which does not necessarily commit her to what we can characterize as an anti-Hirschian position, for she does not confirm that all such illimitable interpretations are to be seen as correct, and indicates quite clearly that there is such a thing as an incorrect interpretation. So far as T. S. Eliot or those Deconstructionists who advocate 'playing with texts' are concerned, it would seem that the very idea of an incorrect interpretation is problematic. If the poem means something to a sensitive reader, then that, Eliot states, is part of the poem's meaning, and the issue of correctness or incorrectness is not raised at all.

At this point the reader may be forgiven for asking what distinguishes T. S. Eliot's implication that an interpretation can approximate to a work's meaning to a sensitive reader, and what in the previous section I discussed as response. The answer would seem to

---

[17] Reprinted in *On Poetry and Poets*, London, Faber, repr. 1969, p.113.

be that whereas Hirsch distinguishes very clearly between response and meaning (by implication if not overtly), for T. S. Eliot response (if of a sensitive reader) may even be seen to form part of meaning. Further consideration of this complex and confused area had better be postponed until my later discussion of 'meaning' – itself a contentious term with reference to literary works. What I hope I have succeeded in doing is alerting the reader to the range of varied and contradictory usages to which the term 'interpretation' has been subjected by theorists.

I will make one final point about interpretation. A number of commentators have pointed out that in their opinion the interpreter should concern him or herself as much with a literary work's gaps and absences as with that which it contains and implies. As the French critic Serge Doubrovsky has put it, literature is made up of as many silences as words, 'what it *says* achieves its full meaning through what it *does not say*: and that is precisely what it *means*.'[18] Writing of D. H. Lawrence's novel *Sons and Lovers* the critic Graham Holderness has suggested that the 'determinate absence' in the work is the bourgeois class,[19] and if true this must enter into an adequate interpretation of Lawrence's work. Sometimes, of course, the absences are only partial, signalling themselves by hints and small clues. Thus although Horace Walpole said he wrote *The Castle of Otranto* 'glad to think of anything rather than politics', André Breton has nevertheless found evidence of contemporary politics in various details of the work.[20]

I should make a few concluding comments on the term 'hermeneutics'. This designates the art or science of interpretation – originally with reference to the study of the Bible, but more recently in a broader sense. 'Hermeneutics' also encompassed the rules, principles and conventions deemed essential for the production of correct interpretations, and the modern use of this term normally invokes this aspect of its meaning. Mention of hermeneutics today normally suggests an appeal to some set of rules governing correct interpretation – not necessarily of literary works.

4 Exegesis

'Exegesis' is another term stemming from a tradition of Biblical study, and it is usually taken to refer to a range of activities from the elucidation of textual cruces and difficulties, through commentary

---

[18] Serge Doubrovsky, *The New Criticism in France*, trans. Derek Coltman, London, U. of Chicago Press, 1973, p.92.
[19] Graham Holderness, *D. H. Lawrence: History, Ideology and Fiction*, Dublin, Gill & Macmillan, 1982, p.12.
[20] See Charles Tomlinson's essay on Coleridge's 'Christabel' in John Wain (ed.), *Interpretations*, London, Routledge, repr. 1961, p.103.

on the implications of textual meaning, to interpretation. The Roman exegetes had the official function of interpreters of such things as omens, dreams, laws, and the pronouncements of the Oracle, so that historically exegesis is very closely linked with interpretation. The most common contemporary use of the term is in connection with the production of annotated scholarly editions of texts.

5 Analysis

'Analysis' is normally engaged in by a critic rather than a reader, for whilst an ordinary reading of a literary text must needs be interpretative to some degree, the analysis of a text involves the relating of textual detail to its effects in a manner not normally compatible with ordinary reading. The literary analyst, like the analyst of a chemical compound or a football match, *divides what is studied into its component parts* so as better to understand its working, structure, or effects. Thus (to oversimplify) while a reader experiences a work as a complex *whole*, the analyst is concerned with the relation of parts to one another and to the totality of their organization.

Now it is clear that reading – especially what I have termed critical reading – can contain analytical elements. Analysis proper, however, normally involves a clear break with conventional reading habits. The analysis of literature can be seen to be analogous to the study of film which works on a frame-by-frame basis, looking at parts which can never be seen in isolation in normal viewing.

I have already noted that T. S. Eliot thought of comparison and analysis as the chief tools of the critic. The virtues of analysis have not gone unchallenged however, and some sceptics have quoted from Wordsworth's 'The Tables Turned' to the effect that 'we murder to dissect'. Because a literary work is far more than the sum of its parts (but is rather the product of its parts) – so the argument runs – then analysis can never come to terms with the fundamental value of literary works. I do not accept this argument in its broadest form, but it has to be said that one of the problems of literary analysis is its throwing of minor details (or possibly minor details) of a work into unexpected prominence. We are back here to the issue of the common reader, who may never be affected by details which the academic critic can isolate and subject to close scrutiny.

Formal analysis is concerned with such matters as prosody, narrative structure, and so on. Such analysis can contribute importantly to interpretative investigation, as it can provide internal evidence for authorial intention and can make generic categorization of a work easier.

6 Appreciation

The word 'appreciation' has an undeniably old-fashioned ring in the context of contemporary critical theory, conjuring up an image of the critic as person who, as Wordsworth sardonically expressed it in the 'Preface' to his 'Lyrical Ballads', has a taste for poetry 'as if it were a thing as indifferent as a taste for Rope-dancing, or Frontiniac or Sherry.' Yet the word has re-emerged in the work of certain recent critics to represent a critical activity that privileges the authority of the text. In appreciating a work a critic seeks by textual study to trace the origin of his or her aesthetic enjoyment. The word has one other semantic attribute that has recommended it to certain critics of late: it implies that textual analysis and textual evaluation are insepara-ble, a position by no means universally accepted by critics. To appreciate a poem or a novel is not just analytically to perceive the work's structure and workings, it is to do this at the same time as one recognizes its aesthetic value. For all that 'appreciation' may con-note the indulgence (and self-indulgence) of the literary gourmet then, it nevertheless points to a particular activity or complex of linked activities in a way that no other term quite manages to do.

7 Discussion

This term, too, has a worryingly general and imprecise ring to many contemporary critics. And yet it is hard to think of a term which captures more precisely what, after all, constitutes a very significant part of literary–critical writing. I am thinking of the sort of critical essay in which a critic moves in and out of the 'world of the work', examining issues and events from the perspective of characters or persona, but then relating these to the world outside the work, considering their implications for (let us say) moral judgement and action in familar everyday life. Take the following brief extract from William Empson's essay 'Honest in Othello', in which Empson is discussing Iago's use of the words 'honest' and 'honesty':

> Iago means partly 'faithful to friends', which would go with the Restora-tion use, but partly I think 'chaste'; the version normally used of women; what he has to say is improper. Certainly one cannot simply treat his version of *honest* as the Restoration one – indeed, the part of the snarling critic involves a rather puritanical view, at any rate towards other people. It is the two notions of being ready to blow the gaff on other people and frank to yourself about your own desires that seem to me crucial about Iago; they grow on their own, independently of the hearty feeling that would normally humanize them; though he can be a good companion as well.[21]

---

[21] In William Empson, *The Structure of Complex Words*, London, Chatto, 1964, p.221.

It is hard to think of a term that better describes what Empson is doing here than the admittedly loose and woolly word 'discussion'. In the present climate of desired scientific rigour in the field of literary criticism loose and woolly terms tend to be frowned upon, but their apparent indispensability may serve to remind us that literary criticism is an impure and pluralistic activity – or, to put it more positively, that literary criticism is not rigorous in the manner of an experiment in the natural sciences, in which a large number of variables can be excluded so that the object of enquiry can be examined in terms of an exclusive and fully-defined set of parameters.

Within 'discussion' I would subsume 'comparison', one of the two 'chief tools of the critic' as I have already quoted T. S. Eliot's saying. 'Comparison' should perhaps merit a separate sub-heading, for its use in literary criticism has important implications. It seems clear from Eliot's essay that the comparison he has in mind is intertexual, that is to say it involves the comparison of one literary work (or part of a work) with another, rather than with something that is not a literary work. I say that comparison has important implications, because to be able to criticize through comparison tells us something about the way in which literary works and our response to them are at least in part constituted by other literary works, by constraints of genre and of tradition. 'To compare' can mean either to observe a similarity or dissimilarity between two things, or to examine their relationship. In the activity of a literary critic both functions can be important ways into the exploration of a work or of a reader's response to a work. When F. R. Leavis compares passages from Shelley's play *The Cenci* and Shakespeare's *Measure for Measure*[22] the contrast allows us more clearly to recognize the weakness and enfeebled Shakespearian echoes in Shelley's work; comparison here can be seen as a form of contextualization that illuminates the weakness of Shelley's writing.

8 Practical Criticism

'Practical criticism' is a particular *technique* of literary analysis, sometimes referred to as 'close reading'. The term stems from I. A. Richards's book *Practical Criticism* (1929). Richards gave a number of his students at Cambridge various poems for discussion, without informing them about the poems' authorship, date of composition, or other contextualizing information. The results suggested to him that his students lacked the necessary skills of evaluative–analytical reading that would have enabled them satisfactorily to place and respond to the poems independent of the missing information. The

[22] In *Revaluation*.

students were unable to discriminate between sentimental rubbish and canonical works, and Richards (and others) concluded that a literary education clearly needed to include far more training in the attentive reading of literary works. The arguments of Richards's book were, arguably, instrumental in revolutionizing literary education, leading to a considerably greater emphasis on the critical reading of individual texts than had hitherto been common.

From this, 'practical criticism' has come to refer to any kind of textual analysis which pays detailed analytical attention to 'the words on the page' of a sort not found in ordinary reading. (It was with this sort of activity in mind that T. S. Eliot referred to the 'lemon-squeezer' school of criticism).

I will say more about such techniques in my next chapter, but I will point out now that although much of the vocabulary associated with practical criticism appears to treat the literary work as an object to be dissected, practical criticism is typically highly *impressionistic*, detailing the subjective responses the text calls out in the reader. At its best practical criticism relates isolable elements in a given text to the subjective responses of the critic in a way that helps the reader to tease out the implications/reverberations of the text in his or her own responses.

It should be stressed that although methods of close reading were developed most of all by the Anglo-American New Critics (broadly defined), and that in some cases these methods were associated with a theoretical position antagonistic to the use of extra-textual evidence in literary analysis and interpretation, since the heyday of the New Critics the techniques have been used by critics by no means sympathetic to such theoretical assumptions. This is a useful example of a critical method surviving independent of the theoretical positions which accompanied its early development.

9 Evaluation

As I will be devoting a later chapter of this book to the question of evaluation, extended discussion of this topic would be inappropriate here. It would be wrong, however, to fail to list it as a crucial 'critical activity', although it should not be assumed that separate listing means that in practice it can be carried out independently of other critical activities.

Let me conclude these introductory comments by stressing that literary criticism is not monolithic, but comprises a range of different activities and functions. When we talk of the literary critic we may naturally think of an academic – but we should remember that book reviewers, publishers' readers, and, indeed, all readers of literature engage in forms of literary criticism. Moreover, those functions and

institutions which we associate with literary criticism are not historically stable, they change and develop. It is important that we keep
sight of the fact that different societies deal with the reading and
study of literature in varied ways: what we may call 'the after-life of
literary readings' takes many different forms and is structured by a
range of different social institutions: publishing, education, journalism, television discussion programmes, and so on. Whereas
today written literary criticism in book and article form is very
intimately related to the academic *study* of literature, in previous
ages in Britain and other countries this was not the case. I suggested
earlier that the narrowing-down of the meaning of the term 'literature' had to be seen in the light of the growing importance of literary
study in the educational system, and the influence of educational
institutions is even more marked with regard to literary criticism.
Indeed, a comparable narrowing down of what is understood by
literary criticism can also be seen to have occurred over the past 150
years, although in a more ambiguous and contradictory way than
with the term 'literature'. Samuel Johnson wrote for educated
readers in general not for university students and teachers, and
although his portrait of the critic Dick Minim is satirical it indicates a
different sort of person and activity behind the satire than would be
suggested by the term 'critic' today.

Were we to ask a recent British or American literary critic what
he or she saw as the function of literary criticism then we might be
told that it was to advance the correct interpretation of literary texts.
It seems highly unlikely that a critic such as Johnson – or Coleridge,
or Arnold – would have been half satisfied with such an answer, for
such critics the criticism of literature was not so much a technical
matter of producing correct interpretations as the exercising of a
social responsibility possessed of inescapably moral and evaluative
dimensions. It is revealing that in recent years such critics have
started to be referred to as 'cultural critics', as if the present usage of
the term 'literary critic' would be misleading if applied to them.

As I have already said, recent literary theory has been dominated
by disputes about literary interpretation; dominated to such an
extent that it might appear that all literary critics do is to interpret
texts and to argue about such interpretations in concrete and in
theoretical ways. But literary critics have done and continue to do
much more than this. They supply or indicate critical contexts for
the reading of literary works, they encourage habits and techniques
of critical reading, they make readers' responses to literary works
more widely available for examination, discussion, and explanation
(by means of textual analyses), they evaluate works and consider
their moral, political, and other implications, they categorize texts
such that potential readers can make informed choices of what to

read and can then read in an informed manner, they attempt to persuade readers to read (or to avoid reading) certain works, they seek to extend the influence and effect of literature (and to study this influence), and not least do they attempt to further political, religious, moral and other arguments and interests through the discussion of literary works.

There are of course problems of boundary definition: what are the lines of demarcation between literary criticism, journalism, reviewing, teaching, studying, and relaxation? There is no one correct answer to such questions; we must recognize that literary criticism exists on a continuum which also includes these other activities, and that the drawing of boundaries involves relatively arbitrary decisions and shifting definitional conventions.

If in one sense there has been a narrowing down and professionalizing of our notion of literary criticism during the present century, in another sense we can say that the last few years have seen the first major setbacks to a process of relatively steady educational and cultural colonialism on the part of literary criticism in Anglo–American society. During the first sixty years of the present century literary criticism – especially in relation to the growth of English Studies – displaced Classics as the central humanist discipline, and in Britain in particular performed a rôle that, it has been argued, was on the European continent performed more by the academic discipline of Philosophy. The twin-pronged challenge of a cultural Thatcherism–Reaganism unsympathetic to the humanities in general, and of new fields such as Media Studies reflective of the relative lessening of literature's cultural hegemony in our society, together constitute the first major check to literary criticism's rising star in the twentieth century.

The modern meaning of the word 'criticism' can be traced back to the later seventeenth century, although the OED gives 1605 as the first recorded date for 'critic' as 'one skilled in literary or artistic criticism; a professional reviewer; also one skilled in textual or biblical criticism.' But the view of the literary critic as sage, social conscience, or moral authority within a culture – a view especially associated with the English critic F. R. Leavis – although it can be traced back to Matthew Arnold or even Johnson or Dryden, achieved its most strident assertion during the present century.

The paradox then, is that at a time when literary criticism became more professionalized and institutionalized and (to oversimplify grossly) restricted itself more and more to textual interpretation, its social and moral claims for its own importance became larger and larger.

II

The Literary Text

'The Text in Itself'

A central point of literary–critical contention in the present century has been the question of whether a literary text can be studied 'in itself'. Critics who believe that it can have been termed 'textual' or 'intrinsic' critics – distinguished from 'contextual' or 'extrinsic' critics. The view of the latter is perhaps summed up in T. K. Seung's argument that it is impossible to provide transcultural answers to the questions, 'what is the intrinsic function of poetry and what are its extrinsic functions?', because the functions of poetry are always culture-bound.[23] The critical grouping most associated with study of the text in itself is that known as the New Critics – an ill-defined 'school', but one to which most agree Cleanth Brooks can be assigned. Brooks has commented on the New Critics retrospectively as follows:

> The one common element that I can discern among those loosely grouped together as New Critics was the special concern they exhibited for the rhetorical structure of the literary text. This emphasis was widely interpreted by traditional scholars and critics as a playing down, if not outright dismissal, of any regard for the author's biography and his place in the culture that nurtured him.
>
> It also implied, many felt, a disregard for the reader and the emotional impact of a given work on the reader's sensibility.[24]

In the retrospective article from which this comment is taken Brooks assures the reader that – popular views of the New Critics notwith-standing – criticism which focuses on the writer's life and back-ground, or on the work that he or she wrote, or on the reader's response to that work, are all 'legitimate modes of enquiry and are compatible with each other'. On the face of it, then, he seems to be advocating a critical pluralism, one which takes account of as many of the components of the literary process as is possible. However, to

[23] T. K. Seung, *Semiotics and Thematics in Hermeneutics*, New York, Columbia UP, 1982, p.118.
[24] Cleanth Brooks, 'In search of the New Criticism', *The American Scholar*, 53 (1), Winter 1983/4, pp.41–53.

this statement of pluralistic tolerance he adds an important rider, that when we come to *interpret* the text then these three modes of inquiry have 'different degrees of authority', and he quotes the well-known warning of D. H. Lawrence's: 'Never trust the artist. Trust the tale. The proper function of a critic is to save the tale from the artist who created it.'[25]

'Trusting the tale' has been recommended by many critics, who in different words have insisted upon 'the primary authority of the text', the need to 'stick to the words on the page' and to 'study the text in itself'. Such advice boils down to a recommendation that one component in the literary process – the text – should have a privileged status, even in some cases to the exclusion of all other components. (The common New Critical conflation of text and work is revealing, as I will argue shortly.) I want to spent some time now looking at the problems that such a recommendation brings with it in practice, for it is a useful illustration of what happens when critics attempt to abstract one of the components of the literary process from the determining context of the process as a whole.

To start with, it seems to me that there is a real problem involved in defining what exactly 'background' or 'outside' information is. If I say that I have severe toothache and you sympathize with me it is arguable that you must be appealing to something outside my experience of pain (which is private and personal to me) to sympathize with me. If we say that such knowledge is merely an aspect of 'knowing the language', that learning a language involves relating common experiences to a shared set of words and expressions, then we still have to admit that different people can know a language more or less well – indeed, that knowing a language better involves precisely that amassing of more 'background' information that is frowned upon by intrinsic critics. So that the distinction such critics make between the (legitimate) need for a sensitive knowledge of the relevant language in order to understand and respond to a literary work, and the (illegitimate) amassing of contextual information for the same purpose, is hard to maintain in practice. As Frank Cioffi puts it in a comment on Wimsatt and Beardsley's 'The Intentional Fallacy':

> No amount of tinkering can save Wimsatt and Beardsley's distinction between internal and external evidence. It isn't just that it's made in the wrong place, but that it is misconceived from the start. A reader's response to a work will vary with what he *knows* . . .
> When is a remark a critical remark about the poem and when a biographical one about the author? The difficulty in obeying the injunction to

[25] D. H. Lawrence, 'The Spirit of Place', in *Selected Literary Criticism*, London, Mercury Books, repr. 1964, p.297.

ignore the biographical facts and cultivate the critical ones is that you can't know what is which until after you have read the work in the light of them.[26]

This is not, of course, to deny that there *is* a problem of relevance; Cioffii certainly overstates the extent to which anything a reader *'knows'* will have the effect of varying his or her response to a work. I have no idea what colour Shakespeare's hair was (does anyone?) but I can't believe that enlightenment on this point would in any way alter my response to his plays. But I can imagine some biographical information that might well do this – of the sort recently explored by E. A. J. Honigmann, for example.[27]

I am now trespassing upon issues that will be dealt with in more detail later on in this book however. I will therefore move on to a further important issue in textual criticism.

Establishing the text

As an undergraduate studying English literature I remember feeling that textual scholarship – the job of establishing or fixing a text – was something that had to be done, but which in an ideal world could be left to our servants to do. But the critical and theoretical issues that such work of textual scholarship both raises and illuminates are crucially important. The questions that a textual scholar has to ask and answer are not on the periphery of literary theory, but lie at its heart. Indeed, the more one reads recent works of textual scholarship the more one wonders whether that easy phrase *'the* literary text' may not be mistaken in many cases. Thomas G. Pavel has reminded us that until recently the centrality of the literary text, as opposed to the romantic centrality of the artist, 'has indeed been the most widespread doctrine in literary criticism'.[28] And that modestly singular form has nestled right at the heart of that centrality. But in the case of so many writers and so many works the use of the singular form raises serious questions: determining what 'the text' is in many cases seems well-nigh impossible.

Now this need not be problematic. But it must be awkward for those who argue that a work of 'great literature' is possessed of autonomy and self-containedness. If you are determined to 'stick to the text', then it is a problem if you are not sure what the text is. (Just as it is more of a problem for a Biblical literalist or fundamentalist if

---

[26] Frank Cioffi, 'Intention and Interpretation in Criticism', repr. in David Newton-de Molina (ed.), *On Literary Intention*, Edinburgh, Edinburgh UP, 1976, p.63.
[27] E. A. J. Honigmann, *Shakespeare: the 'Lost Years'*, Manchester, Manchester UP, 1985.
[28] Thomas G. Pavel, *Fictional Worlds*, London, Harvard UP, 1986, p.8.

the Bible can be shown to contain disputed or unlikely readings; the Apocrypha present more difficulties to believers than to unbelievers).

There are different sorts of textual indeterminacy. Let us list some. (i) We may have a text the words of which we believe to have been corrupted. (ii) We may have several texts and not know which one(s) was/were approved of or preferred by the author. (iii) We may have several texts, all of which were approved of by the author, but in vastly different publishing situations, stages of the author's life and beliefs, socio–historical contexts, and so on. (iv) We may have a variety of texts of which the author clearly ended by preferring one, but which is one that most readers have found inferior to one or more other text(s). (v) We may have one or more texts the words of which have been produced by the admitted author in partial or complete collaboration with other individuals or institutions. (vi) We may have a text which is unambiguously all the author's – but which he or she never looked upon as publishable or finished.

Jerome J. McGann looks at such tricky situations (and others) in his book *A Critique of Modern Textual Criticism.* What is interesting *theoretically* about his arguments is that he is led to attack autonomist theories of literature at various stages of his discussion – including both theories of the autonomous work *and* the autonomous artist. He argues quite directly that 'literary production is not an autonomous and self-reflexive activity; it is a social and an institutional event.'[29] Thus it is impossible to say what an author 'wanted his or her work to be' in isolation: such a question makes sense only when contextualized in various ways – what the author at this time, bearing in mind these publishing possibilities, these constraints, and these collaborations with others, wanted the words on the page to be.

The crucial point theoretically, is that if establishing a text can only be accomplished by appealing to such contextual information, then what sense does it make subsequently to exclude or ignore this or comparable information in reading, responding to, and criticizing the work? How do we defend having recourse to an author's letters, to the testimony of his or her friends, or to evidence of a socio–historical nature to choose between two textual versions of a work, if we then immediately rule such information out of court once we have selected our preferred text? Your former appeal to extra-textual information clearly helps you to read and understand both texts better so as more authoritatively to choose between them; why,

[29] Jerome J. McGann, *A Critique of Modern Textual Criticism*, London, U. of Chicago Press, 1983, p.100.

then, can you not utilize this same information in reading and understanding a single text the status of which is not in question?

The same argument in a slightly different form arises when the author's own extra-textually stated preferences are used to decide which text is to be preferred of two or more available. Why should such a category of information be valid to *choose* but not to read and interpret a text? And if T. S. Eliot is right that an author is only another reader of his or her work,[30] then why should he or she be allowed to choose the preferred final text? Moreover, is a textual variant 'text' or 'background'?

McGann points out that many literary works cannot be said to exist in one text which unambiguously represents its author's 'final intentions', and, moreover, that even though a manuscript may represent what an author in one sense clearly wanted to write, it may not represent what he wanted to publish. McGann associates the appeal of the 'final intentions' argument with 'the concept of the autonomy of the creative artist', an autonomy he is quite sceptical of. So far as a work is concerned, he argues that

> an author's work possesses autonomy only when it remains an unheard melody. As soon as it begins its passage to publication it undergoes a series of interventions which some textual critics see as a process of contamination, but which may equally well be seen as a process of training the poem for its appearances in the world.[31]

Arguments such as this have important implications for our understanding of such concepts as 'authorial intention', at which I shall be looking in more detail later on in this book.[32] In passing, however, it is worth noting that McGann finds the concept of 'final authorial intention' to be 'a deeply problematic concept'[33]; although it may well seem clear and simple with regard to more recent works, it is far less so in practice.

Before we move on, however, one of McGann's conclusions seems to be to merit repetition. According to him, narrowly to identify a literary work with an author and, as a result, critically to simplify the author's identity, have the result that

> the dynamic social relations which always exist in literary production – the dialectic between the historically located individual author and the historically developed institutions of literary production – tends to become obscured in criticism. Authors lose their lives as they gain such critical identities, and their works suffer a similar fate by being divorced from the social relationships which gave them their lives (including their

[30] see no.17.
[31] McGann, p.51.
[32] See pp.71–80.
[33] McGann, p.68.

'textual' lives) in the first place, and which sustain them through their future life in society.[34]

This conclusion seems to me to be in line with my own view of the necessity of the critic remaining aware of all the components in the literary process, and of their dynamic interconnections.

Even those who do not consciously hold to an autonomist theory of the literary text often assume that if we have a literary work then there must, ideally, exist a perfect text (and one only) which represents that work – even if the recovery of this text is impossible. It is this assumption which I wish the reader to question. Let us take a specific example – Coleridge's poem 'The Rime of the Ancient Mariner'. There is an interesting (if eccentric) introduction to some of the textual problems of this work by William Empson, who notes that

> The chief difficulty in arriving at the right text for *The Ancient Mariner*, a splendid poem which was much mangled by its author for reasons of conscience, is that though he made harmful changes where he had fallen out of sympathy with its basic ideas he kept improving it in detail, even to the first posthumous edition (1834). One needs therefore to form an eclectic text, always considering the motives of the author in his successive changes, and only rejecting those which conflict with the basic impulse and conception of the poem.[35]

This 'eclectic text' is a text that Coleridge never saw or approved, but which contains nothing that at one time or another he did not write. Clearly it is a *choice* rather than a discovery of the editors, one which is as much critical as scholarly. Note how Empson's insistence on 'the motives of the author in his successive changes' places the text in a particular context of determining forces rather than seeing it as autonomous and ideal.

There were (and are) many critics who objected strongly to the text of 'The Rime of the Ancient Mariner' produced by Empson and his co-editor (and the two editors themselves parted company at one point). The lesson for us is that there are certain major (or 'great') literary works which can never be limited to a single perfect text; their life as works straddles two or more texts, and this plural textual existence draws valuable attention to the links a work has with the other components in the literary process, the links which autonomist theories of the text (or the author) conceal or deny. Those who read Charles Dickens's *Great Expectations* in an edition which prints the alternative endings for the novel which Dickens wrote may regret knowing of one of the alternatives, but once they know of it they

[34] McGann. p.81.
[35] William Empson and David Pirie (eds.), *Coleridge's Verse: A Selection*, London, Faber, 1972, p.27.

cannot remain unaffected by it, cannot unproblematically consign it to an extra-textual limbo.

The claims for unity and autonomy

One issue which arises naturally out of a discussion of textual scholarship is that of the work's unity and completeness. There are many examples of writers publishing works to which they subsequently added, such that a problem arises as to whether the first-published version can be said to be complete or possessed of artistic unity. Artists very often have the cynicism of parents when it comes to the well-formedness and completeness of their offspring; there is a nice anecdote about the painter Braque being arrested in an art-gallery when discovered putting the finishing touches (or perhaps just some additional touches?) to one of his displayed canvases. It is generally readers and critics rather than writers who have insisted upon unity and completeness as attributes of a work, although they have been joined by some writers.

Clearly this issue is related to the issue of textual autonomy, for if something is autonomous then there is a good basis for claiming that it is complete and that it forms a unity. Indeed, it seems possible that the claim for autonomy can be seen as an ill-judged extension of the claim for unity, that attempts to defend the work's autonomy have had at base the desire to argue for its unity.

It is revealing that it is to works of art in particular that the claim for unity has been applied. We see arguments for the unity and completeness – even self-sufficiency – of philosophical treatises, mathematical proofs, and scientific explanations, but it is noteworthy that in such circumstances people use phrases such as 'It's a work of art'.

The idea that literary works are or should be characterized by their unity is an old one. In his *Poetics* Aristotle argued that

> just as in the other imitative arts the object of each imitation is a unit, so, since the fable is an imitation of an action, that action must be a complete unit, and the events of which it is made up must be so plotted that if any one of these elements is moved or removed the whole is altered and upset.[36]

It is not hard to see how such an argument could encourage autonomist theories of the literary work. Something with unity seems complete in itself, whereas (as I have pointed out in relation to 'The Rime of the Ancient Mariner') something that is in some sense not absolutely finished and complete reminds us of its links with what is

[36] Aristotle, *Poetics viii*, trans. L. J. Potts, Cambridge, Cambridge UP, 1958, p.28.

outside it. If a defining characteristic of unity is completeness – 'No more, no less, in no different form or arrangement' – then readers and critics may easily be tempted to suggest that the ideal work can be fully appreciated in itself, independent of further knowledge or information. But surely this is to confuse two quite separate things: what the *work* needs, and what a *reader* needs in order to read the work. Because formalistic theories of literature tended to subsume the reader into the work this crucial distinction was passed over, and it was assumed that if the work was satisfactorily complete then the reader could read, respond to and interpret it with no recourse to any extra-textual information. This seems to me to be clearly wrong – and at the very least some extra-textual things are undeniably essential: a reader with a set of reading abilities, and a context which allows him or her to read the work.

I have said that the idea that literary works are or should be characterized by their unity is an old one, but I should add that it is by no means an unchallenged one. During the present century in particular – and especially with reference to what we can call modernist literature – a rival set of assumptions or beliefs has arisen. According to this general perspective nothing in life is characterized by complete unity and so, if literature is to emulate, reflect or portray life accurately (and I will have more to say on this later), then neither should literary works be seen or desired to possess perfect unity. The argument is not logically watertight: there is no reason why a unified work may not make us think about or recognize a disunited world. But the ideas of imitative form which recur in different versions from age to age have perhaps been responsible for the view that if one feels life to consist of chaotic and unfinished episodes and experiences then the works of art which attempt to capture and analyse life should emulate this apparent disunity.

As I have suggested, the issues of 'unity' and 'autonomy' are very closely interrelated in literary–critical discussion, and those critics who argue for the literary work's autonomy seem to be drawn to works possessed of a striking unity, a unity which, in a way paradoxically, involves highly complex connections and patterns of influence and dependence *within* the work. In this view there are few, or no, points of determining contact between text and non-text, but within the work itself all is relationship and mutual influence. The literary text comes to resemble a fortified medieval town from this perspective: foreigners and outsiders are repelled, or allowed in only after rigorous checks, but within all is bustling life; exchange, mutual interdependence and influence are the rule.

In order to distinguish between the different sorts of unity enjoyed by literary works Coleridge's distinction between mechanic and organic form is of some use. I shall be addressing the issues raised by the form–content distinction in more detail later, but would point out at this stage that the sense of completeness produced by certain formal arrangements can contribute to a work's apparent unity. According to Coleridge mechanic form involves the 'impressing' of 'a determined form, not necessarily arising out of the properties of the material', while organic form 'is innate; it shapes as it develops itself from within, and the fullness of its development is one and the same with the perfection of the outward form.'[37] Coleridge's distinction seems to conform with the varying accounts of the writing of literary works given by different authors; some adapt to a pre-existing structure or pattern, while others find that, as Virginia Woolf reports of the writing of her novel *Mrs. Dalloway*, 'the idea started as the oyster starts or the snail to secrete a house for itself.'[38]

The concept of unity has very often been associated with that of organic form: the close, internal interdependence of the parts and levels of the literary work suggesting an analogy with a living being, and living (especially human) beings being seen to possess a unity and autonomy, standing apart and protecting themselves from their environment. And yet, it is worth reminding ourselves, organic bodies are actually *more* dependent upon their environments than inorganic matter. Without the possibility of negotiated and controlled exchange with their environments organic bodies perish: a fact which should perhaps cause us to rethink the simple assumption that the more a work is possessed of unity, the more autonomous it is.

Consideration of different literary works quickly reveals that they are possessed of varying degrees and types of unity, and of a greater or lesser independence of a particular environment. A standard test for unity involves the removal or rearrangement of parts of a work, something which has a disastrous effect on some works and relatively little on others (think, for example, of Daniel Defoe's *Moll Flanders* and Emily Brontë's *Wuthering Heights* – or Byron's 'Don Juan' and Keats's 'Ode to a Nightingale').

Pre-existing views – either of formal structure or of a story – can influence our sense of a work's completeness or otherwise. A poem that resembles a sonnet but has only thirteen lines, or a novel about a voyage in the *Titanic* that ends before the loss of the ship, will inevitably seem incomplete.

This apart, it does seem to be the case that readers actively search for unifying elements in literary works, in the sense that they try to

[37] S. T. Coleridge, *Shakespearian Criticism*, ed. T. M. Raysor, Cambridge, Mass., Harvard UP, 1930, p.224.
[38] Virginia Woolf, 'Introduction' to the Modern Library Edition of *Mrs Dalloway*, New York, Random house, 1928, p. viii.

discover *consistency* and *completeness* in a work. Where a work appears on first acquaintance to involve contradictory elements or loose ends then it seems that readers attempt to discover deeper or more general themes or patterns so as to subdue such wayward elements or to indicate their more fundamental conformity. Thus, for example, many of the terms much loved by the New Critics – 'tension', 'paradox', 'ambiguity' – were utilized to suggest that apparent disunities were only elements in a larger unity. But at this point we may pause to ask to what extent unity is in the eye of the beholder – whether it is the reader's active search for unifying elements and principles rather than the work's intrinsic unity that is in question. This question impinges upon issues to be considered in our later consideration of the rôle of the reader, but some preliminary comments are in order here. Clearly a reader's expectations are of crucial importance to the reading process, and a reader who searches for unifying elements in a work while ignoring or playing down discordancies and incompletenesses may be said to impose a kind of unity on a work rather than discovering one in it. Unity would thus be as much a product of the reading process as a quality of texts if this were true. Wolfgang Iser's analysis of the reading process, for example, uses as analogy two people looking at a night sky: both see the same stars, but they 'see' different figures by joining the stars up in alternative ways.[39] George Eliot gives us a comparable image in her novel *Middlemarch*: a pier-glass of polished steel will have minute scratches running in all directions, but illuminated from one perspective the scratches will arrange themselves in a fine series of concentric circles. Are many allegedly textual qualities such as unity actually products of a particular reading process?

In part, yes. But we must also recognize that finding unity is much more difficult with regard to certain works than to others: if unity were all the reader's doing there would, we assume, be no ununified works.

A key issue here is that of closure; that sense we get from certain literary works that the work is complete, that nothing is missing. In his Preface to *Roderick Hudson* Henry James suggests that

> Really, universally, relations stop nowhere, and the exquisite problem of the artist is eternally but to draw, by a geometry of his own, the circle within which they shall happily *appear* to do so.

Such a desire for strong closure can be contrasted with the wish testified to by other writers to achieve the opposite effect, to use the literary work as a springboard into those unstopping relationships in the life beyond the text. A comparison of the openings and

[39] Wolfgang Iser, *The Implied Reader*, London, Johns Hopkins UP, 1972, p.282.

endings of novels shows how much different authors vary in their wish for artistic closure; some beginnings and endings remind the reader of those Jamesian universal relations – including those between the work and the world – and some try to obscure or disguise these.

Accordingly, we get a sense of closure, completeness, and thus unity from works which seem to complete a particular pattern, to cover a specific period of time, for instance, as with Joyce's *Ulysses* or Woolf's *Mrs Dalloway*, or to 'enclose' the action of a work by a sudden time-shift – as at the end of Keats's 'The Eve of St. Agnes'.

So far as autonomy is concerned, perhaps the most telling argument against it is the linguistic one. Literary works are ineluctably linked to the world outside them by the language in which they are composed. However unified they are, they do not exist for the person who has no linguistic access to them, an access founded upon that person's socialization into a particular speech community. Without that umbilical cord of language, literary works would be still-born, enjoying only the autonomy of death.

Form, content, genre

A traditional way of analysing a literary work is by means of a distinction between its form and its content. Although apparently simple and unproblematic at first sight, this distinction turns out to be neither of these things upon closer examination. This is firstly because different critics mean different things by 'form', and secondly because both 'form' and 'content', when used of a literary work, denote aspects of the work that are mutually interdependent and incapable of existing alone. Let us look at these issues more closely.

'Form' can refer either to a generic category – 'the novel form', 'the sonnet form' – or to a work's organizing principle and mode of presentation. Thus Coleridge's previously mentioned distinction between mechanical and organic form involves the second of these two conceptions of form.

Moving to my second point, it is not just of literary works that we can note the interdependence of form and content. A proposal of marriage can be delivered in a variety of forms – written, by telephone, kneeling in front of the recipient, and so on. In one sense, what we have here could be termed a variation of forms involving the same essential content. But the nervousness indicated by the addition of the adjective 'essential' draws attention to an obvious point: the variation of forms necessarily involves some variation in content. The meaning of a proposal of marriage delivered (without pressing reason) by telephone is different from one made in person: form seeps into content; only in limited and artificial situations can the form of a message be treated as a neutral carrier – and certainly not in the case of literature.

In the case of many forms of human communication the verbal element is only a part of the total message: with direct interpersonal communication, for example, paralinguistic elements form an essential part of the communicative material. With literature (leaving aside the complex issue of performance, which I will address in section VI) we have, at first glance, only words. It is for this reason that the force of the appeal to consider only 'the words on the page' is so strong with literature; a literary work survives through time and is disseminated as an organization of words, in one sense there would appear to be nothing else. In spite of the strength of this appearance, a literary work is actually more than words on the page. And the simplest way to demonstrate this is by showing how the same set of words can assume a different significance. At the most basic level, this can be done by spatial rearrangement of words – setting poetry as prose or vice-versa. The way words are set on the page creates patterns which are not, strictly speaking, verbal. It is not a *verbal* feature of the sonnet that it has fourteen lines, it is a *formal* feature. Form, in other words, cannot exist for a literary work without words, but it is not itself a verbal matter.

A somewhat more sophisticated example would involve the attribution of given formal qualities to a work by the means of what we can call its aesthetic packaging: presenting the same words but in such a way as to suggest that the formal intention behind their composition is different. Even such simple matters as book cover designs and back-cover blurbs can lead to the same arrangement of words being read rather differently, and generic misattributions can have a major effect on the understanding of 'the words on the page'.

I have already suggested that 'form' and 'genre' are not easily separable concepts, and certainly in some usages the two are more or less synonymous. Generic distinctions often involve the isolation of formal qualities, and many of the terms used to analyse literary works have both formal and generic implications – 'metre', 'plot', 'narrative', 'action', and so on. In general terms we can suggest that the word 'genre' evokes a more social and institutional context of meaning than does 'form', although this is not universally the case. But one cannot imagine a writer successfully inventing a genre for him or herself; for a genre to exist some form of reader recognition, of social acceptance, is necessary. We could use the parallel of 'dress' and 'uniform'; anyone can create and wear a new form of dress – and the people he or she meets will be affected by this dress and will be influenced by it (perhaps) in estimating him or her as a person. But for a form of dress to become a uniform, other people have to recognize it as such. Thus when (after the success of the

Beatles' Sergeant Pepper) teenagers started wearing cast-off uniforms as a form of dress, mistakes were made, as they sometimes are with literary works. But army uniforms would not work as uniforms unless people apart from the wearers knew what a uniform was and what in general it tended to signify. Such ignorant people might be affected by a uniform as dress, but not as a uniform. In like manner, any new literary form can have an immediate effect upon readers, but generic constraints and significance work only for those who recognize the genre. I will come back to the issue of genre; now I wish to say more concerning form.

A key – and recurrent – idea in literary criticism is that of sympathetic or appropriate form: the form echoing, complementing, or indicating the content in some manner. On a simple level this can be seen wherever the means of literary expression in some way mirror or fit in with the abstractable content of what is said. Take for example the gloss F. R. Leavis puts upon two lines from Keats:

> And sometimes like a gleaner thou dost keep
>   Steady thy laden head across a brook . . .

> In the step from the rime-word 'keep', across (so to speak) the pause enforced by the line-division, to 'Steady' the balancing movement of the gleaner is enacted.[40]

'Enacted' is a favourite word of Leavis's, and implies an appropriateness of fit between form and content – to express the matter crudely. Particular verse-forms arguably match given sorts of subject matter better than others: the self-enclosed rhyming couplet with its firm closure suits well a bluff optimistic outlook composed of monadic items of belief, whereas the freer verse-form of 'The Prelude' is clearly more appropriate for the more wandering linear development of Wordsworth's narrative of growth. In general the more rigid the form the easier it is to distinguish form from content: to use Coleridge's distinction again, the more mechanical the form the more it can be distinguished from literary content.

The way in which 'form' slides into 'genre' is another reminder of the social and institutional dimension of literary identity. To revert to my dress analogy, although there clearly is a sharp dividing line between 'dress' and 'uniform', there is a gray area in between the two which we can term 'style'. The thing about a style is that it has a range of social meaning; a style is not a style unless it is recognized for what it is, even though to be stylish a person has to display individualistic and personal skill in dress (unlike with the wearing of a uniform). In like manner, on that continuum which has form at

---

[40] *Revaluation*.

one end and genre at the other, there are aspects of literary organization and production which involve both conventions available to a reading public and the personal and creative manipulation of these conventions. The thing to remember is that, as Jerome McGann has already been quoted as saying, literary composition involves *negotiation* between an individual writer and social institutions, pressures, traditions. A wide range of different external pressures can shape literary material, giving it a particular form but allowing the writer to respond creatively with his or her own style. And formal elements can very quickly assume generic significance: as commentators have wryly remarked, the more inescapable the pressure to conform to a particular style of dress for a given group, the more that style starts to resemble a uniform.

What are the factors that can exert formal pressure on a work, that can be instrumental in creating and defining a genre? It is worth listing these, particularly as some commentators have suggested rather too narrow a range of factors involved in generic classification.

subject
setting
theme
authorial attitude
genesis
purpose
occasion
structure
effect

The list is by no means complete; other commentators have included psychological and sociological factors as well as historical specificity as criteria for the definition of a literary genre. Literary works are categorized into genres by means of varying criteria: *Hamlet* is both a tragedy and a play. Moreover, genres are not fixed and stable entities; new genres emerge and encompass previously written works, the definition of older genres alters over time. Thus at the time she wrote her last poems Sylvia Plath was unaware that she was writing what would become classified as confessional poetry; William Empson's book *Some Versions of Pastoral* widened the definition of what a pastoral was.

In addition to the categories given above, we should remember that such things as the technological and economic exigencies of publishing can also influence literary form. Writers in the nineteenth century published novels in instalments because that was an economically successful and established way of publishing novels. However, a novelist who knew that he or she was going to write a novel which would be published in instalments could choose to compose it in such a way that it would be appropriate for this form of publication. This is why it is interesting to know where the original instalment divisions in a work such as Henry James's *The Turn of the Screw* were: it gives some explanation of narrative crises which otherwise seem rather crude and unproductive. In its original instalment publication, James was able to turn a mechanical requirement into a more organic aspect of his novella's form. The work's subsequent publication in book form (albeit revised by James) gives us a not unusual example of a work which in its final published version is possessed of a form which has been partly created by now invisible pressures.

With the theatre in particular, this sort of constraint may be especially noticeable. There is a limit to what an actor can remember, what a stage can contain, how long an audience can sit in their seats.

Whatever the causes or origins of generic or formal characteristics, their function within the literary process is crucial, for they influence the expectations that a reader brings to a literary work. In her useful introductory book *Genre*[41], Heather Dubrow starts by quoting the opening of a literary work (one which she has created herself), and points out that we read this quite differently if we believe we are starting a detective novel from the way we would read it were we convinced that we were starting a *Bildungsroman*. Form and genre help us to categorize literary works, and thus inform us of the sort of reading, the sort of response that is likely to be appropriate to a given work. Of course a writer may wish to modify or even to frustrate our expectations, but even in such cases the expectations are in a sense relied upon by the author. (Although this raises the interesting question of the different readings successive generations of readers give to the same work, as works become recategorized generically and as the idea of what constitutes a particular generic category changes.)

It is important to remember however that in very broad terms we can say that form or genre can determine our expectations for two rather different reasons. A given genre may have a *conventional* or an *intrinsic* significance. Let us take an example. If one started to read a poem which opened with the words, 'There was once a Prime Minister named Thatcher', then one would be pretty confident that what was likely to follow would be unlikely to be complimentary. This is because the line follows the pattern of a conventional limerick opening, and limericks are not conventionally associated with serious poems offering praise of the individual(s) discussed, but with light or bawdy topics frivolously or scandalously treated. To write a serious or devotional poem in the limerick form would involve an

[41] London, Methuen, 1982.

enormous struggle against the force of an unvarying weight of tradition. But even if this tradition were non-existent, a contemporary poet who invented the limerick form would find that it had certain intrinsic unsuitabilities for the exploration of serious or complex issues. The sense of rapid acceleration and unreflective closure induced by the verse-form does not naturally lend itself to a developing and subtle questioning of a serious topic. It is intrinsically unsuitable for such a use. The conventional significance of the limerick form can thus be seen to have something to do with its intrinsic qualities.

Particular genres are characterized by their requiring adherence to a given set of *conventions* governing not just formal matters but also content in many cases, as well as such things as modes of publication or delivery, interpretative strategies, and so on. (The list I gave earlier on covering the range of factors involved in generic classification will suggest other conventional restraints – occasion, for example.) Such conventional restraints may be either flexible or restrictive; formulaic genres have by definition quite restrictive conventions, experimental works normally abide by generic conventions in a very loose and unrestrictive manner. Thus it is more or less impossible to imagine a Mills and Boon romantic novel with a tragic ending, or one in which evil triumphs. Fomulaic literature has been associated in particular with popular or folk art through the researches of individuals such as Vladimir Propp, but it is important to remember that other genres can display strongly formulaic elements – think of opera. The appeal of the formulaic is an interesting topic for investigation. On the one hand it is clearly the case that particular forms of oral delivery in illiterate communities encourage formulaic art, which is easier to compose, to receive, and to understand in such circumstances. Because of the high level of redundancy involved, the memory and attention of a listening audience are not unduly strained. The pleasure derived from formulaic literature may be complex: in part the reiteration of familiar patterns which have a clear function with regard to social cohesion and ideological persuasion; in part the recognition of significant or skilled variations within the narrow limits of the allowable.

In general we can suggest that social stability or even stagnation encourages fixity in generic and formal conventions, and that rapid social change or overt conflict is often associated with generic instability. Moreover, while generic fixity grants a close writer–reader relationship at the expense of writer experiment, the collapse of generic reliability gives the writer great freedom at the expense of a loss of contact with his or her readers.

Movements such as these raise a number of interesting theoretical questions. I have already mentioned that shifts in genre categories and conventions bring with them questions about the extent to which different readers carry alternative expectations with them in reading certain works. We could cite the gradual acceptance of modernist conventions (or anti-conventions): a British sixth-former studying Eliot's 'The Waste-Land' can hardly be said to be approaching it in the same way as a reader in 1922.

When we turn to the reasons for generic development and change, two different theories of the dynamic behind such change can be advanced. I have already suggested a more open, social explanation: generic conventions are linked to social conventions, both ideologically and also in as much as they reflect the realities of writer–reader relationships, relationships which are stable in periods of social stability and are disturbed by social change. Other commentators have suggested a more internal and closed set of reasons: in his essay 'On Realism in Art' Roman Jakobson argues that the longer conventions of representation last, the more automatic and undemanding habits of artistic perception become. At this stage the artist feels the need for a new convention: the artist-innovator 'must impose a new form upon our perception, if we are to detect in a given thing those traits which went unnoticed the day before'.[42] Virginia Woolf makes a very similar suggestion in her essay 'Mr. Bennett and Mrs. Brown'. After drawing a comparison between social conventions (as, for example, those which govern behaviour at a party) and literary conventions, she argues that when a convention ceases to be a means of communication between writer and reader but rather obstacle and impediment, then 'the feeble are tempted to outrage, and the strong are led to destroy the very foundations and rules of literary society.'[43] Changes in social conventions are here seen not as cause but as analogy: we have revolutions in literature just as (but not necessarily because) we have revolutions in society.

The constraints offered by a particular genre may either be welcomed or regretted by a writer: fixed conventions may offer either a useful framework guaranteeing contact with a readership, or a bar to the discussion and representation of serious issues.

Generic classifications tend to be both *descriptive* and *prescriptive*, but at different times one or other of these elements may predominate – sometimes very considerably. We can link this to the fact that generic classification may precede or follow the writing of a work; it may be imposed upon a work *post facto* by a critic, or the writer may

---

[42] Roman Jakobson, 'On Realism in Art', trans. Karol Magassy, in Ladislav Matejka and Krystyna Pomorska, *Readings in Russian Poetics*, London, MIT Press, 1971, p.40.
[43] Virginia Woolf, 'Mr. Bennett and Mrs. Brown', repr. in *Collected Essays*, vol. 1, London, Hogarth Press, repr. 1971, p.334.

have had a clear sense of generic constraints as he or she started to write. Very often descriptive classifications tend to harden into prescriptive ones, as with the neoclassic interpretation of classical 'rules'. Since Plato and Aristotle a tripartite generic division of literature has held considerable sway, and still can be seen in the classification of literature courses at colleges and universities: poetic or lyric, epic or narrative, and dramatic. Along with such exercises in classification has gone a traditional opposition to the mixing of genres, that process of descriptive categories becoming prescriptive ones of which I have already spoken.

A consideration of formal and generic issues reminds us that a literary work is never perceived innocently by a reader; to talk of seeing a literary work as it 'is' is to ignore a range of problems arising out of variations between different reader expectations, variations which in part at least can be related to changing literary conventions, developments in our generic categories.

III

Language

Literary works are the only art-works which consist largely of language – if one interprets 'literary work' in such a way as to include such things as oral poetry and some of the performing arts. It is not surprising, therefore, that theorists have sought to use ideas about language in the construction of theories about literature.

Speaking very generally, we can divide such linguistic approaches to literature into two major types: those which use the nature and study of language as a *model* for investigation into literature, and those which consider language as the *medium* of literature and which consequently argue that the more we know about language in general (or about the particular sort of language which is said to characterize literature) then the better able to understand literature we will be. I would like to spend some time discussing aspects of these two general approaches in view of their importance in contemporary theory.

In the present century both Structuralist and Post-structuralist theorists have based their view of literature on (among other things) the drawing of an analogy between literature and language. As one commentator puts it, for the structuralist literature 'is organized at every level *like* language, and it is a central part of structuralist purpose to reveal the similarity.'[44] It should be stressed, however, that such views of the organizational similarity of literature and language are associated with one particular linguistic theory or paradigm, that which is based to a large extent upon the work of Ferdinand de Saussure, whose lectures were published posthumously in reconstructed versions produced by students of his and entitled *Cours de Linguistic Générale*. Saussure's main contribution to linguistics lay, arguably, in his distinction between synchronic and diachronic approaches to the study of language, that is between language studied either as a complete system working as such at one point of time in a given language community, or language studied in its development, historically.

[44] Ann Jefferson, 'Structuralism and Post-structuralism', in Jefferson and Robey, p.87.

The distinction has been very productive heuristically, as it has suggested a convenient division of labour for researchers. Synchronic linguistics has also led to the synchronic study of other systems of meaning, including that of literature (i.e. 'literature' understood as a system for generating literary meanings within a particular reading community). A further very influential distinction of Saussure's was that between *langue* and *parole* – between the whole abstract *system* which allows for the generation and understanding of utterances, and the *actual utterances* so generated and understood by concrete individuals. (The distinction has much in common with the Chomskeyan distinction between *competence* and *performance*.)

Linguisticians influenced by Saussure concentrated upon the construction of grammars which would depict and reproduce the 'abstract system of language' as it existed at a particular point in time. Those working in other fields have used comparable points of departure to investigate complete meaning systems: the anthropologist Claude Lévi-Strauss pioneered the study of human cultures in this way, for example. So far as literature is concerned, the intention has generally not been to examine individual literary texts, or to suggests rules for such an examination, but to investigate systems of 'literariness' which make the writing and reading of literature possible. Jonathan Culler puts this position clearly:

> Just as sequences of sound have meaning only in relation to the grammar of a language, so literary works may be quite baffling to those with no knowledge of the special conventions of literary discourse, no knowledge of literature as an institution.
> . . .
> In the case of literary criticism it is . . . true that once we are no longer attempting to analyse a corpus of works but are seeking to describe the ability or competence of readers, we shall find our methodological situation considerably improved.[45]

The word 'competence' gives some clue of the likely provenance of Culler's theoretical position here.

Moreover, just as the linguistician may use his or her own linguistic competence as object for analysis (as it is argued that all native speakers share a comparable competence *vis-à-vis* their own language), so too, argues Culler, can the investigator into literature, 'as a reader oneself . . . perform all the experiments one needs.'[46]

If I can now shift into a rather more critical gear, I would like to suggest that this particular tradition includes interpretations of Saussure which are controversial – either in terms of their correct

---

[45] Jonathan Culler, 'Prolegomena to a Theory of Reading', in Susan R. Suleiman and Inge Crosman (eds.), *The Reader in the Text*, Guildford, Princeton UP, 1980, pp.49, 50.
[46] Culler, p.51.

representation of Saussure's position or in terms of their truth. For example: Saussure saw synchronic and diachronic approaches to the study of language as complementary:

> Speech always implies both an established system and an evolution; at every moment it is an existing institution and a product of the past. To distinguish between the system and its history, between what it is and what it was, seems very simple at first glance; actually the two things are so closely related that we can scarcely keep them apart.[47]

Saussure stresses that one of the tasks of linguistics is 'to describe and trace the history of all observable languages',[48] and he argues that 'one must sense the opposition between the two classes of facts [i.e. those produced by historical and by synchronic investigations] to draw out all its consequences'.[49]

I insist on this point because many of Saussure's declared adherents have represented Saussure's position to involve the *displacement* of historical linguistics by synchronic study of language. This is particularly important in one context. What everyone with only a passing acquaintance with Saussure's ideas knows is that Saussure declared the linguistic sign to be arbitrary: there is no *necessary* link between sign and referent, or between signifier and signified (that is, between the sound 'tree' and the concept of a tree). Some commentators have used this as a basis for cutting language away from reality entirely, for assuming that there is no fixity of meaning in words, which can mean what we like. In a chapter on modern linguistics and the language of literature David Robey, for example, uses this aspect of Saussure to defend a Deconstructionist 'playing with texts'; Saussure's concept of the arbitrariness of the linguistic sign is the base upon which statements such as the following are built:

> This . . . postulate, the most radical and fertile feature of Saussure's thought, rests on the idea of an essential disjunction between the world of reality and the world of language.

> . . . instead of things determining the meaning of words, words determine the meaning of things.

> . . . if the literary text is seen as a sign or set of signs in the Saussurean sense, then its meaning or content must be the product of a structure of relationships or differences whose connection with the 'real' world is purely arbitrary.[50]

[47] Ferdinand de Saussure, *Course in General Linguistics*, ed. Charles Bally and Albert Sechehaye, trans. Wade Buskin, London, Peter Owen, rev. ed. 1974, p.8.
[48] Saussure, p.6.
[49] Saussure, p.83.
[50] David Robey, pp.39, 46.

I cite the third extract for the second time to explain why I am spending so much energy arguing about an interpretation of Saussure's linguistics in a book concerned with literary theory. Saussure is here used – and is used by many other theorists arguing a similar case – to justify a procedure that denies any link between the literary text and the real world (I believe in the real world well enough to be able to dispense with the use of quotation marks here).

But if we turn back to Saussure (or, at least, the text that we have to represent his opinions), this is what we can read:

> . . . the thing that keeps language from being a simple convention that can be modified at the whim of interested parties is not its social nature; it is rather the action of time combined with the social force. *If time is left out, the linguistic facts are incomplete and no conclusion is possible.*[51] [my italics]

As Thomas G. Pavel has put it, the principle of arbitrariness maintains only that there is no motivated link between the conceptual side and the phonetic side of a linguistic sign, 'it does not deny the stability of linguistic meaning, once the semiotic system has been established.'[52] 'Playing with texts' will, therefore, have to find other theoretical foundation than that provided by Saussure.

Literary theorists who have argued for language as a model for literature have ended up, in many cases, advancing positions which can be categorized as highly formalistic and idealist. Literature (or the literary text) can – the argument runs – be treated as 'context-free'; it can be studied independent of its origins – and indeed the whole concept of 'origin' is seen to be highly dubious.[53] The text is free-floating, untouched by purposive human activity and expression or by the interpretative conventions of groups or reading communities. Such ideas seem to recur regularly in theoretical discussion, but especially during the present century. They can be found in writings by the Russian Formalists, the Anglo–American New Critics, and in Structuralist, Post-structuralist and Deconstructive theorizing, although often coexisting or battling with opposed views. I cannot help wondering whether what we have in such instances is actually a reflection of the *social* isolation of the theorists concerned: cut off from social power or responsibility, feeling (correctly) that their own views are in a sense arbitrary, they project this situation on to language in general or literature. While I am on this point I will add that those who talk of 'playing with texts' (I include those influenced by Roland Barthes and Jacques Derrida among others) rarely take account of actual study of play, study which reveals a dependence upon concrete social existence rather

[51] Saussure, p.78.
[52] Pavel, p.3.
[53] See my subsequent discussion, pp.67, 68.

than arbitrariness and unfettered freedom and independence.

The development of Structuralist (and other) theories of literature which made use of Saussure very often built upon applications of Saussure's ideas in other intellectual areas, especially Anthropology; the work of the Frenchman Claude Lévi-Strauss was especially influential in this respect. It is arguable that much in Structuralist and Post-structuralist literary theory bears the marks of this genealogy. In the early part of the present century Anthropology was dominated by Western-European studies of 'primitive societies'. The perspective was very much that of a detached and superior outsider, relatively uninterested in the origins of what was being observed, but concerned with its present workings as a complete system studied scientifically, and often not aware that what was seen as an 'objective' view was actually saturated with ideological and cultural presuppositions. Much the same can be argued about more recent defences of playing with texts, except that it can be argued that they misrepresent their object far more seriously. Let us return to the linguistic analogy. How helpful it is to see the literary work as analogous to a sentence (Todorov actually compares characters and actions in a narrative to nouns and verbs at one point)? There are, I wish to argue, serious problems with this assumption. Firstly, we need to recognize that the analogy between 'knowledge of a language within a given language community (*langue*)', and (to requote Culler) 'knowledge of the special conventions of literary discourse', is less than watertight. Within a given language community there will be differences of spoken and written competence, variations in terms of accent, register, and dialect, and greater and lesser degrees of competence *vis-à-vis* the manipulation of the language. But there *is* a common *langue*; in Chomskeyan terms all adult members of the language community share a common competence to generate and comprehend grammatical utterances.

It is hard if not impossible to isolate a comparable literary competence – hard at the level of reception, impossible at the level of production. To put it another way: we know that all adult native speakers of a particular language must share a common, internalized 'grammar' which enables them to generate a perpetual stream of grammatical utterances and instantly to recognize diversions from grammatical correctness (the existence of variations within, say, English, is a complicating factor, but one that does not disprove this point). But two professors of English Literature may well disagree about interpretative rules with regard to literature, both so far as single works or whole genres are concerned. To take an example: the interpretative problems posed by modernist literature in its early years find no convincing parallel in shifts in language conventions or grammar. Language changes, but not in such a way that suddenly a whole group of English speakers find that they can't understand what another group of English speakers – whom they understood a few years before – are saying.

Moreover, although it has certainly been illuminating to view formulaic literature in terms of an assembling of components chosen from a fixed store in a manner akin to the assembling of a sentence from a store of parts of speech, it seems less and less likely that it is equally illuminating to view literature which is less obviously formulaic in the same way. As I have already mentioned, although it may seem natural to us to talk of the 'meaning' of a literary work there are actually significant problems associated with this formulation. A literary work does not, it has been countered, possess a 'meaning' in the way that a sentence is possessed of a meaning. Alternative ways of approaching literary works suggest that it may be far more fruitful to see literary works as objects for interpretation, as means whereby the creative imagination is exercised, as forms of self-expression, as artifacts to be appreciated, as ways of reflecting or commenting upon the world, or as carriers of ideological significance.

There is little doubt that so far as literature is concerned Structuralism's greatest success has been in the study of narrative – 'narratology'. Here the use of the linguistic analogy has been, I think, fruitful and illuminating, and has generated the possibility of a far more detailed, accurate, and probing discussing of narrative choices made by authors or found exemplified in texts. Why is this? Because, I think, that as in the case of a sentence grammar, we are talking about a system involving the significant choice and combination of items from a finite store. But once we move into the realm of literary response, or interpretation, then we move beyond the point where talk of selection and combination from such a finite store is helpful or illuminating.

Two final comments on this topic. Firstly, that it seems revealing that although such attempts to provide a linguistic model for the study of literature start very often by talking of the need to focus attention on to 'literariness' or the competence of literary readers, before long such enterprises turn their attention to the interpretation or study of individual literary texts, so that we start to see books with titles like *Post-Structuralist Readings of English Poetry* appearing on the shelves. To me this suggests that there may be insuperable problems facing the successful completion of the original project; whether interpretations of individual texts can be seen to follow on from the investigation into literary competence is highly disputable. My second point is that I do think that a concern with the linguistic analogy did lead many critics to pay far greater attention to problems associated with readers, readings and audiences. This attention is clearly in tension with the view of literary works as occupying a different, and separate, level of reality from the real world.

Turning to views of language as the medium of literature we might feel ourselves to be on safer ground. Surely literary texts consist of language, it is above all words in a certain selection and combination that writers can be said to produce. Nevertheless many commentators have suggested that it is highly misleading to refer to language as the medium of literature in the way that we might refer to stone as the medium of sculpture. Stone is not naturally expressive, language is. A sculptor thus transforms something that is not naturally expressive into something that is, whereas a writer manipulates something naturally communicative to generate the literary work. Moreover, whereas the sculptor does not represent stone in his or her work, the writer very often (but not always) does represent language. Hamlet's soliloquies consist of the language of Shakespeare's text which represents the language spoken by Hamlet.

When a sculptor starts work on a piece of sculpture it is arguable that he or she has some idea in his or her head of what the piece is to look like, which he or she then uses the available stone to create and represent. (Clearly it is more complex than this; the sculptor will in part find out what the piece must be in the course of working on the stone.) But a writer can have no idea in his or her head which is totally independent of the words that will be used to bring the literary work into being. Writing a literary work does not involve a writer who knows what he or she wants to say going to a stock of words for the first time and picking out the ones to be used. A writer may, of course, start with an image: many writers have said that they do. But this image will very soon assume a verbal identity – it may indeed be a verbal image from the start.

What I am arguing against is the idea that writers possess pre-linguistic ideas of what they want to write and then express these ideas in words. To a greater or lesser extent the words *are* the ideas. In his essay 'Tragedy and the Medium' the critic F. R. Leavis attacked the philosopher George Santayana's use of the word 'medium' in the course of a discussion of tragedy. According to Leavis,

> to demand that poetry should be a 'medium' for 'previously definite' ideas is arbitrary, and betrays a radical incomprehension. What Mr Santayana calls 'Shakespeare's medium' creates what it conveys; 'previously definite' ideas put into a 'clear and transparent' medium wouldn't have been definite enough for Shakespeare's purpose.[54]

[54] F. R. Leavis, 'Tragedy and the Medium', repr. in *The Common Pursuit*, Harmondsworth, Penguin, repr. 1966, p.124.

A number of attempts have been made to characterize literature by means of its alleged use of a particular sort of 'literary language'. In many versions of this argument the case is limited to poetry: writers as widely different as Thomas Gray and the Prague structuralist Jan Mukařovský have advanced the theory that poetry is characterized by a particular sort of language use. According to Gray, the 'the language of the age is never the language of poetry; except among the French, whose verse, where the thought or image does not support it, differs in nothing from prose.'[55] For Mukařovský, 'the function of poetic language consists in the maximum of foregrounding of the utterance'[56]: by 'foregrounding' is meant a form of de-automatization whereby language is no longer a transparent means to a particular meaning, but is itself contemplated as language.

The problem with such views is that whenever they have appeared it has been only to be refuted: it seems that there is no form of language use which is intrinsically unusable in literature or in poetry. Mukařovský's formulation might be said to be noteworthy in as much as it fixes not so much upon language but upon the *function* of poetic language, thereby opening the door to an involvement of the reader as well as the language itself. But even here, it is hard to find a particular attitude towards language that is common to all literary reading: the claim that this necessarily involves foregrounding is hard to sustain unless one resorts to manoeuvres such as that of representing *Tristram Shandy* as a typical novel – a sleight of hand of which the formalists have been accused by at least one commentator. A wider claim is the traditional one that there is such a thing as an aesthetic attitude proper to works of art, and to be distinguished from other attitudes by means (primarily) of its disinterestedness. Such views are more properly considered in my later section on reception, but I will remark at this point that I am not alone in finding the claim that works of art or literature should appropriately be considered in a disinterested or 'aesthetic' manner to be at best a problematic one.

So far as the view that literature can be defined in terms of a certain sort of language – 'literary language' – is concerned, this seems to me to make the essentialist mistake of assuming that defining a literary work is like defining what 'gold' is, something to be tackled by means of the analysis of 'the thing itself'. As will be apparent by now, my own view is that literature can only be

---

[55] From a letter to Richard West, 1742. Repr. in Edmund D. Jones (ed.), *English Critical Essays*, London, OUP, repr. 1965, p.265.
[56] Jan Mukařovský, 'Standard Language and Poetic Language', repr. in Paul L. Garvin (ed.), *A Prague School Reader on Esthetics, Literary Structure, and Style*, Georgetown UP, 1964, p.19.

understood in terms of the whole literary process: its definition has to be at least partly *institutional*. I say 'at least partly', because I do believe that literary works must have some intrinsic qualities (or perhaps, better, potentialities) that enable them to perform a function as part of the literary process. In this respect literary works are unlike chess pieces or monetary tokens, the physical manifestation of which is more or less totally irrelevant to their institutional function. We could play chess with buttons or carrots, but in practical terms we could not successfully treat a guide to home computing as a literary work.

One of the things that can be said of literature from a linguistic point of view is that it represents one of the most context-independent forms of written language we have. No literary work is completely independent of context: we have to know what a literary work is to be able to read one, to make a simple point. But most written forms of language rely far more than does literature upon context: writing is not supported by those paralinguistic features which grant speech a higher redundancy rate and thus greater freedom from misinterpretation, and so writing is usually aimed at a particular audience – whether defined temporally, geographically, socially, or whatever. Socrates, in Plato's *Phaedrus*, points out that written compositions do not know how to address the right people and not address the wrong; for this reason writers normally try to arrange that only the right people read what they write. But literary works are probably read by a wider range of different people at varying times and in numerous places than any other written documents – with due exception for works such as the Bible. Now because context often limits ambiguity or misinterpretation, this means that literary works may be vulnerable to a range of misinterpretation or attributed (unintentional) ambiguity not suffered by most other written documents.

As a result, the study of ambiguities in literary works, of varied forms of multiple meaning involving connotations, paradoxes, ironies and so on, raises certain problems. Are such multiple meanings 'in the work', or are they a function of the work's lack of a determining context? Can ambiguities be seen to be intrinsic to a text, or must they be related to an author's intention – or unconscious creation?

The study of ambiguity has played an extremely important part in the literary criticism of the twentieth century: unlike the recipients of letters, the interpreters of legal documents, and the readers of works of History, Philosophy, or Science, literary critics have declined to find multiple meanings in a literary work undesirable, but have often argued that they constitute part of the richness of literature and generate profundity rather than confusion – although the opposite virtues of simplicity and straightforwardness have also been admired. A key figure here is clearly William Empson, whose multiple readings in *Seven Types of Ambiguity* have had a profound effect on literary-critical thought. In more recent years the issue has been more that of rival interpretations of a single work that multiple readings which constitute part of the richness of a single interpretation. This takes us straight to some central debates about the acceptability of plural readings and interpretations. According to Jonathan Culler, 'the single most salient and puzzling fact about literature' is that 'a literary work can have a range of meanings, but not just any meaning.'[57] This of course is not just an issue involving verbal ambiguity, but verbal ambiguity is implicated in it, and it raises central questions about what language is and how it works on and through us. Can an utterance have meaning independent of an intention to mean? Is there such a thing as unconscious meaning? I will be looking at such issues in subsequent pages, but I want to stress that these are not just problems of genesis or reception; they also involve questions about the nature of language itself.

Literature is *written*. This simple fact has a number of important implications which need to be mentioned at this stage. The written form of literature is clearly a stabilizing factor: we can have fixed (or relatively fixed) texts to study – unlike the situation with regard to oral poetry or narrative where the same text is never delivered twice. This fixity may be a very important factor for the study of literature (we can read a critic's comments secure in the knowledge that he or she has read the same words as we have read), and writing can be said to have granted verbal art the same advantages of fixity as had previously been limited to the plastic arts. But the comparison carries with it some warnings: language is not so stable or unvolatile as is stone or paint: languages are only apparently unchanging – historical study reveals that they are in a state of constant development. The oral poet and his or her audience share the same language: the writer and his or her reader often do not, and the differences may be both obvious and also unnoticed. The English Shakespeare wrote and spoke resembles our own in many ways: we can understand much without recourse to a dictionary. In an obvious sense it is our language. And yet not only have the meanings of words undergone subtle changes in many instances, but forms of address, registers and other language variations are governed now by different conventions. 'The words on the page' are the same, but unless they are understood in context their meaning may have altered.

The written form of literature imposes a necessarily linear pattern on literary works or, at least, of our initial experience of them. With a

[57] Culler, pp.51, 52.

play, a poem, a novel, we start at the beginning and work through to the end. Paintings and statues do not have beginnings and endings, even though their contemplation takes place in time. Five people looking at a painting will not stop looking at it at the same point: five readers of 'Resolution and Independence' will – at least on first reading – all finish at the end of the last line. This means that all readers of works of literature experience common patterns of temporal succession in their responses. Variations in reading are possible – I will talk about them in a later section – and we may all *remember* a work in different (and non-linear) ways. The New Critics in particular were fond of referring to literary works as objects (urns or icons), and their discussions often zig-zagged between the linear reading experience and the 'well-wrought urn' as the literary work appeared in memory.

Because the author controls the *sequence* of experiences/ideas the work provides the reader with, he or she has considerable power: we have to experience a literary work in the order the author wants us to experience it, and most readers are under the sway of the convention that forbids us to skip passages or peek at the ending of a novel too soon. But it does mean that we can make a distinction between 'the work as experienced' and 'the work as remembered', such that talk of 'the work' may fail to represent the complexity of the literary work's mode of being. I shall return to this issue in section VI.

The written form of language is not a simple transcript of its spoken form. Because speech leaves no reliable permanent record it generally has a higher level of redundancy than writing, so as to guard against errors of interpretation. Speech is also accompanied by paralinguistic features – tone, register, accent, and so on – which help to prevent mistakes and which combine with spoken language to produce subtleties of meaning. In person-to-person dialogue such things as posture, gesture, facial expression, eye-contact, and so on are also crucial to effective communication. Writing in contrast (at least today) tends to use more standardized forms; it is often hard to tell a person's dialect from their writing. And in writing pauses, hesitations, repetitions – all these disappear. The playwright will try to allow for their use in performance; the poet may use metre and rhythm (and even rhyme) to evoke their presence in the reader, and the novelist too may attempt to indicate their presence in speakers by direct comment or by sentence structure and punctuation. For a writer to evoke the sense of spoken language demands skill: writing is more naturally adapted to the account than the experience. Thus the writer who wishes to represent or suggest human life in its entirety is faced with the problem that many human experiences are not primarily or significantly verbal. Non-verbal experiences then must be translated into words – something that is hard to do without apparent artificiality, as Dostoyevsky points out in his novella 'A Nasty Story':

> Everybody knows that whole trains of thought can sometimes pass through our heads in the twinkling of an eye, like so many sensations, without being translated into any kind of human, much less literary, language. But we shall try to translate our hero's sensations of that kind and present to our readers at any rate the substance of them, what were, so to speak, their most essential and plausible aspects.[58]

In this respect, then, it may be acceptable to refer to language as a literary medium, for just as stone represents for the sculptor that which is not stone, so too language can represent or evoke for the writer (and the reader) that which is not in essence verbal. In other ways, however, the formulation is unsatisfactory and potentially misleading: so far as literature is concerned language is as much what is represented as the 'medium' for that representation.

[58] Fyodor Dostoyevsky, *The Gambler/Bobok/A Nasty Story*, trans. Jessie Coulson, Harmondsworth, Penguin, repr. 1986, p.195.

IV

Genesis

The question of where literary works come from has been treated by some critics in the manner that the Victorians were alleged to treat the question of where babies come from. That they had to come from somewhere was admitted, but that one had to pay much attention to the question of origins was not. In general terms we can agree with Leszek Kolakowski that

> the question of whether or not the knowledge of genesis is indispensable in understanding the 'structure' is wrongly put. It simply depends on what we are asking. There are many questions which we can try to answer without genetic enquiry and many others which require a genetic explanation.[59]

Interestingly, however, the understanding of works of art is seen by Kolakowski to fall into the latter category. To understand works of art we have to understand their conditions of birth, how and why they were created, responding to what personal and social pressures, in the teeth of which constraints and oppositional forces. That mobility of which I spoke in the previous section is something of which, in this view, we should be suspicious – as suspicious as we would be of a person whose history was a closed book to us.

The issue has divided twentieth-century literary critics down the middle, between those who demand that the literary work be treated as independent and free-standing, and those who insist that unless it is seen as the final and visible stage of a long and complex process of creation then it cannot properly be understood. (The dispute is often widened to include other contextual elements as well as those relating to the work's genesis). Behind this polarization are some complex issues. Let us look at some of them in turn.

The author

Most literary works have single authors. That is to say, the name of

[59] Leszek Kolakowski, 'Althusser's Marx', in Ralph Miliband and John Savile (eds.), *The Socialist Register 1971*, London, Merlin, 1971, p.126.

one person usually appears on the title page of most novels, collections of poems, and plays. It is true that a certain degree of collectivity may be concealed behind such attributions of authorship: friends who have read the manuscript, audiences which have responded to earlier readings of poems, editors who have suggested major or minor additions or deletions, and even censors who have blue-pencilled or altered substantial parts of the text. Such contributions are the rule rather than the exception, and yet even so literary works are far more the product of individuals than are television programmes, films, or oral compositions relying heavily on traditional stories and modes of expression. Even painters and sculptors frequently use apprentices for journey-work, while musicians (along with dramatists) are dependent upon performers. Few artists are so much in sole command of their creations as are writers, even though writers are dependent upon a complex social structure of publishers, patrons, libraries, booksellers, educational institutions (readers must be able to read), and so on.

On the face of it this ought to make literary works easier to understand. A number of different people with varied skills, intentions, and artistic vision may have created a film: the film may reflect the tensions and conflicts of its production. But with a literary work surely we should be able to go to one man or woman and settle any problems of interpretation.

Yet the relationship between an author and his or her work is often far from simple. Whereas in everyday life if we do not understand a statement we naturally turn to the person who uttered it to clarify its meaning, in the case of a literary work it seems to be the case that there are many questions that the creator cannot answer (given that he or she is available to be asked questions), and there are many questions to which authors can be claimed to have given the wrong answer.

I used the word 'meaning' above, and I should here repeat that it may well be misleading to reduce all problems of literary response or understanding to 'meaning': it seems likely that the verbal form of literature may seduce us into treating literary works like statements or propositions – something we are less tempted to do with paintings or statues.

One of the first commentators to draw attention to the unreliability of authors as explicators or interpreters of their own work was Plato: W. K. Wimsatt and Monroe Beardsley quote Plato in their influential article 'The Intentional Fallacy' to the effect that when the poets were asked about the meaning of passages in their works, there was 'hardly a person present who would not have talked better about their poetry than they did themselves. And then I knew that not by wisdom do poets write poetry, but by a sort of genius and inspiration.'[60]

Much more recently William Empson has commented on one of his own poems that, 'I can't say what this poem means, partly because I don't remember, partly because I don't want to, and partly because it doesn't matter since the poem failed to say it.'[61] We have, then, a number of reasons already why an author may not be the best person to ask about his or her work. If the work's composition involved some form of inspiration or possession then the author will be no more able to explain the work than any other reader; the author may have forgotten what he or she was trying to do in writing the work, or may have something to conceal – or may recognize that the work does not incorporate or engender what it was originally designed or intended to do. These are all reasons for treating what an author says or thinks about his or her own work with caution. A critic may, however, try to relate a literary work to an author's life, experience, and intentions independently of the author's own opinions of such relationships. We have, therefore, two rather different ways of taking the authorial genesis of a work into account in literary criticism, and we should bear this in mind and try to avoid confusing what are, essentially, different critical procedures.

I have mentioned W. K. Wimsatt and Monroe Beardsley's article 'The Intentional Fallacy', and it seems the case that so far as Britain and the USA are concerned there is no single piece of argument that has had so profound an effect on the discussion of literary genesis as has this article. The thrust of Wimsatt and Beardsley's argument is towards the treatment of the literary work as independent of its author – who is adjudged to have no greater interpretative authority with regard to his or her work than any other competent reader.

> The poem is not the critic's own and not the author's (it is detached from the author at birth and goes about the world beyond his power to intend about it or control it). The poem belongs to the public.[62]

Wimsatt and Beardsley are in distinguished company. T. S. Eliot argued, a decade before 'The Intentional Fallacy', that the poem was not what the poet 'planned' or what the reader conceived, and that

---

[60] Wimsatt and Beardsley, p.7.
[61] Quoted by John Haffenden in his Introduction to William Empson, *The Royal Beasts and Other Works*, London, Chatto, 1986, p.20. In a contribution to a special edition of *Agenda* on Criticism, (14[3], Autumn 1976), Empson suggests rather wickedly that the reason American Lit. Crit. theorists put a veto on consideration of the author's intention was that 'they are all descended from Germans . . . and no German has ever understood the intention of an English writer' (p.24).
[62] Wimsatt and Beardsley, p.5.

its 'use' was not restricted to what the author intended or to what it actually did for readers.[63] Much later, commenting upon a book of interpretations of poems including one of his own, he noted approvingly that

> the analysis of 'Prufrock' was not an attempt to find origins, either in literature or in the darker recesses of my private life; it was an attempt to find out what the poem really meant – whether that was what I had meant it to mean or not.[64]

Recent discussion concerning 'The Death of the Author' is really a continuation of issues that have been implicit in much literary-critical debate for a very long time, but which have been foregrounded in the present century in particular.

Different literary-critical theories have, however, condemned the author to death in a variety of ways. Whereas the New Critics accepted that the author lived while he or she engaged in literary composition, but lost all parental rights once the literary child was born, more recent Deconstructionist and Lacanian theories have, in what has been termed the rejection of 'the humanist conception of the subject', argued that the author as traditionally conceived never existed. What lies behind such arguments is the belief that the humanist conception of the subject sees individual subjectivities as monadic and self-determining, as an indisputable point of *origin* in a world of mediations, determinations, and influences. The Deconstructionist view is that to privilege the individual as point of origin is to ignore the fact that individual subjectivities are products as much as points of departure, made as much as (if not more than) making. For such critics, then, the individual author is site rather than source – the battleground upon which rival influences and forces clash, and from which victorious troops march on to effect changes in the world.

Such a view clearly has much in common with traditional Marxist views of the misguidedness of seeing the individual as the source of history rather than admitting that it is 'the motor of the class struggle' or 'the clash between productive forces and productive relations' which creates rather than is created by individual human beings and their subjectivities. But Deconstructionist views go beyond such a formulation in a number of ways. Firstly, traditional Marxist views do admit the existence of individual consciousness and subjectivity, but grant it a subordinate rather than a privileged rôle in social life and historical determination. Several versions of Deconstructionism deny that individual subjectivity describes any

[63] T. S. Eliot, *The Use of Poetry and the Use of Criticism*, London, Faber, 2nd ed. 1968, p.31.

[64]*The Function of Criticism*, p.113.

meaningful reality (not too difficult to do when variants of the same position are denying that language refers to anything outside itself anyway). Secondly, such views deny the existence of *any* privileged point of origin: so far as the literary work is concerned, there is no author/authority to appeal to; all we have is the endless play of signifiers, locked in an eternal childhood in which no stern parental voice ever calls them in to get washed and go to bed.

These argued positions, in consort with less extreme attacks upon the authority of the author, have had the virtue of calling attention to the dangers of treating the individual writer as conscious master of his or her own creativity, and have turned attention to the ways in which social, historical, ideological forces may use the writer as scribe, may speak through him or her. Deconstructionist views tend to be more universalistic and less interested in culture or history – displaying here evidence of their Freudian provenance (ironically, in view of the attitude towards the issue of origins found in Deconstructionist writing).

My own position is that whilst I agree that there is no ultimate point of origin, no privileged source which has absolute priority in interpretative disputes, nonetheless the world is full of determinations, and the free play of the signifier, paradoxically, *reintroduces the subject by the back door*. For what is the free play of the signifier but the privileged individual interpreter, possessed of the absolute freedom to interpret as he or she will that Deconstructionists have previously characterized as the humanist conception of the subject? There may not be a single privileged point of origin, but there are determining forces, and these exist in a hierarchial structure. Even if we treat the individual author as site rather than source we still have to describe how one site varies from another, and after a while such an enquiry comes precariously close to admitting that the individual acts as one of a number of points of origin and influence, even if not an absolute one or a creator who is lord of all he or she surveys. For myself, to talk of 'the author' is not necessarily to deny that what he or she writes is primarily determined by extra-individual forces in some or even all instances. (That this is the case on occasions is not, as I have tried already to suggest, a particularly new argument.) But it *is* to assert that individual consciousness, however determined and formed, exists. Not only exists, but exerts a significant and crucial force during the process of literary composition in many cases.

Can a literary work mean something independently of what its author wanted it to mean? Some of the most extreme disagreements between literary critics in the present century have been engendered by this question, with Wimsatt and Beardsley and other formalists answering 'yes', and the American critic E. D. Hirsch answering 'no'. I will discuss these opposing views at greater length later on in the present section, but before doing so it is worth asking to what extent different answers to the questions may be appropriate in the case of different works and different authors.

It certainly seems to be the case that the creative process varies very considerably from one writer to another and, perhaps even more revealingly, from one age to another. Thus in general terms we can say that the notion of inspiration was treated with scant respect by many writers in rationalistic eighteenth-century England, whilst it was almost an item of faith for the Romantics. Samuel Johnson treated with scorn the opinion of Thomas Gray that he (Gray) could write only at happy moments: an opinion which Johnson dismissed as a 'fantastic foppery'.[65] Johnson's own view was that 'a man may write at any time – if he will set himself *doggedly* to it.'[66] The Romantic poet Shelley, in contrast, stated bluntly that 'Poetry is not like reasoning, a power to be exerted according to the determination of the will.'[67]

It would be unhelpful merely to enquire whether Johnson or Shelley was correct: the evidence supports the assumption that Johnson described his own experience of composition, and Shelley his. It is, incidentally, perhaps revealing that although a contemporary of Johnson's, Thomas Gray wrote poetry that seems transitional between Augustanism and Romanticism.

In the present century we seem to find both Johnsons and Shelleys: Wimsatt and Beardsley quote an account by the poet A. E. Housman which runs as follows:

> Having drunk a pint of beer at luncheon – beer is a sedative to the brain, and my afternoons are the least intellectual portion of my life – I would go out for a walk of two or three hours. As I went along, thinking of nothing in particular, only looking at things around me and following the progress of the seasons, there would flow into my mind, with sudden and unaccountable emotion, sometimes a line or two of verse, sometimes a whole stanza at once.[68]

I cannot resist adding another anecdote concerning the varied stimuli different writers required to help them compose; in his biography of D. H. Lawrence Harry Moore reports that Lawrence's friend William Hopkin once inadvertently heard a Mrs Dax tell Mrs Hopkin: 'Sallie, I gave Bert [i.e. Lawrence] sex. I had to. He was over at our house, struggling with a poem he couldn't finish, so I took him upstairs and gave him sex. He came downstairs and finished

[65] See Johnson's *Life* of Gray.
[66] See Boswell's *Journal of a Tour to the Hebrides*, entry for Monday, 16 August.
[67] See Shelley's *A Defence of Poetry*.
[68] Wimsatt and Beardsley, p.8.

the poem.'[69]

Whereas some writers plan their work out very carefully before they begin writing, others do not. In his novel *Tristram Shandy* Lawrence Sterne has his narrator declare that when a man sits down to write a history, 'he knows no more than his heels what lets and confounded hindrances he is about to meet with in his way', and he declares that

> But this is neither here nor there – why do I mention it? – Ask my pen, – it governs me, – I govern not it.

It seems likely that, given a time-machine, it would be more profitable to ask Johnson about his works than to make a similar enquiry of Shelley. It is worth noting, incidentally, that as R. A. Sharpe has pointed out, some qualities in art-works necessarily involve reference to their authors: 'irony', 'satire', and 'wit', for instance.[70] If an author honestly believes at the time of writing that he is not being satirical then it seems difficult to see how one can claim that the work is satire, unless one posits an unconscious or dictating Muse with a satirical intent of which the author is unaware.

Many nineteenth- and twentieth-century authors have talked about the independence their works – or characters – have had of their own conscious control. Pushkin commented on his character Tatyana in a letter, remarking that she had shown Eugene (another character) the door, and that, 'I simply would not have believed her capable of such a thing.'[71] D. H. Lawrence commented upon Clifford Chatterley's incapacitation (in *Lady Chatterley's Lover*) that 'The story came as it did, by itself, so I left it alone.'[72] Thomas Hardy surprised a number of people by constantly talking of his character Tess as if she were a real person. And Luigi Pirandello dramatized the situation in which an author's characters develop lives and wills independent or his or her own in the play *Six Characters in Search of an Author*. None of this should be taken to mean that the authors concerned did not have to work long and hard to produce their works – they did; but this work seems to have involved the setting down and organization of impulses that came at least partly involuntarily.

Given what I have just reported concerning D. H. Lawrence's compositional methods it comes as no surprise that Lawrence advised against allowing authors a privileged status with regard to

[69] Harry T. Moore, *The Priest of Love*, London, Heinemann, rev. ed., 1974, p.112.
[70] R. A. Sharpe, *An Introduction to Contemporary Aesthetics*, Brighton, Harvester, 1983, p.113.
[71] Quoted by Sharpe, p.123.
[72] Quoted by Ricardo J. Quinones, *Mapping Literary Modernism*, Guildford, Princeton UP, 1985, p.178.

the interpretation of their own works:

> The artist usually sets out – or used to – to point a moral or adorn a tale. The tale, however, points the other way, as a rule. Two blankly opposing morals, the artist's and the tale's. Never trust the artist. Trust the tale. The proper function of a critic is to save the tale from the artist who created it.[73]

Many writers have spoken of literary composition in terms of the entering of a strange and separate world, or in terms of a sort of dream experience. Coleridge's account of the writing of his poem 'Kubla Khan' and of the effect of an interruption from 'the person from Porlock' is oddly similar to Joseph Conrad's description of a similar interruption to his writing of his novel *Nostromo*.[74]

Moreover, many critics have pointed out that a writer's consciously held views (whether or not these refer directly to works written by the writer in question) can be a very bad guide to the full appreciation of the writer's work. A number of critics have argued that there is implicit in Dickens's later novels a more and more radical critique of Victorian society, even though these novels were written at a time when Dickens's consciously held views were become more and more conservative and dismissive of radical social views. We have, however, reached the stage at which we should turn to consider the much-debated issue of authorial intention.

Intention

So central has argument about authorial intention been to literary-critical discussion over the past four decades that the authors of the polemical article 'Against Theory' have taken the 'issues of belief and intention' to be paradigmatic for literary theory as a whole, and have assumed that to demonstrate the misguidedness of discussion of this topic is effectively to demonstrate the redundancy of literary theory.[75] This is an extreme position, but it does draw our attention to the remarkable centrality of discussion of intention to literary theory since the publication of 'The Intentional Fallacy' in 1946. How do we explain the enormous interest in this issue?

At the heart of the debate lies a concern for *authority*: to which Court of Appeal can we have recourse in the event of a dispute concerning a work's interpretation? Some such authority was, more and more critics became convinced, necessary to resolve the more

---

[73] See note 25.
[74] Coleridge's account is published with 'Kubla Khan' in his *Poetical Works* (ed. Ernest Hartley Coleridge, OUP, repr. 1967). Conrad's account comes in *A Personal Record* (Dent Collected Edition, pp.98, 99).
[75] See note 7.

and more unresolved interpretative debates that raged in a time of rival orthodoxies. Without a Court of Appeal, more and more of these debates would remain unresolved. And whatever theoretical arguments they adduced, the anti-intentionalists started off from a firm belief that statements of authorial intention did not constitute a satisfactory Court of Appeal. The pro-intentionalists, in contrast, have set off from the fixed conviction that the author represents an essential – or even the only – Court of Appeal able to solve interpretative disputes; without recourse to the testimony of his or her intentions we will sink into interpretative anarchy. The debate has, in its turn, led to a consideration of whether this latter state of affairs would be a bad thing: *should* we aim at uniformity of interpretation?

Other factors also conspired to focus debate on to the topic of intention in the years immediately following the Second World War. Treating the literary work as object, as thing-in-itself to be analysed independent of its origins, was seen by many to raise literary study to the level of the physical sciences at a time when the humanities seemed to be losing intellectual centrality and status in the west. And anti-intentionalism also flourished during the years of the Cold War, in topical opposition to the Marxist insistence on the importance of a work's genetic context, and seemingly offering the chance to treat the literary work as a free-standing unit in a manner comparable to the way in which individualist ideologies demanded freedom for the human individual. The reader was left free to interpret the work unhindered by Big Brother author.

In retrospect, much of this debate has involved a progressive sharpening of our understanding of the complexity and variation involved in the concept of authorial intention. We now realize, I think, that it is naïve to assume that an author can intend a literary work in the way in which I can intend a simple verbal utterance. For a start, when I intend a remark to inspire, or wound, or cheer up someone, my intention is directed *at a particular person in a particular communicative situation*. If someone else, the next, day, asks me what I intended by my remark they mean 'What did you intend with regard to the person to whom you uttered this remark?' But when a reader of *Bleak House* asks what Dickens intended in writing the work the scope of the question is more diffuse, involving not a time-limited utterance to a particular person but an intention somehow covering innumerable readers at different times in different places.

Now a law can be said to have an intention behind it even though it too is aimed at many different people similarly separated in time and space, but no law has been intended to apply to the range of individuals who have read or witnessed *Hamlet*. And laws, we should remember, are regularly reinterpreted in the light of changed circumstances: a law passed in the nineteenth century referring to vehicles will be taken in the twentieth century to refer to motor-cars even if the framer of the law had no conception of a motor-car and so could not possibly have intended to refer to one.[76] But whatever literary intention is or can be, it clearly must be unlike the intention behind the framing of a law: the vast majority of writers just do not have so concrete and delimited a notion of what it is they wish to effect *vis-à-vis* their readers as does the person who frames a law – who, anyway, wishes to include many who never read the law within its scope.

According to Wimsatt and Beardsley in 'The Intentional Fallacy', 'Intention is design or plan in the author's mind.' They proceed to the claim that intention 'has obvious affinities for the author's attitude toward his work, the way he felt, what made him write.'[77] Quentin Skinner has pointed out, usefully, that we can distinguish between 'motives for writing' and 'intention in writing',[78] which sharpens up Wimsatt and Beardsley's formulation considerably. Samuel Johnson claimed to have written *Rasselas* to pay for his mother's funeral, but clearly that was his motive for, rather than his intention in writing. We should note, too, that an author can have a design or plan in his or her mind without being conscious of the fact – one of the reasons why the issue of 'unconscious intention' can be raised. Moreover, we must assume that Wimsatt and Beardsley's formulation does not necessarily exclude the possibility of an author's intention developing as the work is written: a design or plan is usually subject to modification in the light of experience. What *is* involved in the formulation, however, is the assumption that in some way or other the design or plan is separate from the intention as embodied – the work itself.

But is the view of intention as 'design or plan' adequate? After all, the framer of a law may have a design or plan in his or her mind prior to the writing of the law, but his or her intention is surely prior to that design or plan. ('Design' is confusingly ambiguous: do Wimsatt and Beardsley mean 'chart, model' or 'intention' when they use the word 'design'? One presumes the former: it would be tautological to define intention as 'intention in the author's mind'.) I *intend* to stop people drinking and driving, as a result I *design* a law to prevent this. My intention is what I want the law to achieve: is literary intention

---

[76] Although E. D. Hirsch, in writing subsequent to his two major books on interpretation, has tried to argue that an author can intend what is unknown to him or her but nonetheless entailed by his beliefs and intentional acts.

[77] Wimsatt and Beardsley, p.4.

[78] Quentin Skinner, 'Motives, Intentions and the Interpretation of Texts', in Newton-de Molina, p.216.

what a writer wants a work to achieve, or effect in readers? If so it is hardly a design or plan.

Even when we take additional comments by Wimsatt and Beardsley into account, problems remain. An 'author's attitude to his work, the way he felt, what made him write' – all these could be argued to be circumstantially rather than necessarily related to intention if intention is 'intention in' rather than 'motive for', and if intention includes a concern to affect readers in certain ways.

Of course, a work may be affected by the writer's motive for writing. *Rasselas* may bear signs of its having been written hurriedly. E. M. Forster claimed that he wrote partly in order to win respect; presumably he did not want readers of his novels to remark that here were novels that gave signs of having been written for this reason, but such signs there may nonetheless be in his work.

By common consent then, authorial (literary) intention differs from other sorts of intention. The writer often has no clear sense of what he or she wishes to effect in his or her readers in the way that the framer of a law has. Literary intention matures and changes as a work is written: anyone who has studied successive versions of a literary work in manuscript will have realized that authors change their mind about what they are doing (or, perhaps, that the work changes direction, and that the writer must abandon false starts and *cul-de-sacs*). Intentions have to be studied historically as well as perceived synchronically; what McGann has argued of texts is true far more of intentions – they change and develop.

We should remember too that it is common to see literary composition in terms of the writer's expressing him or herself: that suggests a different sort of process, with different 'intentions', than is involved in the framing of a law or a proposal of marriage.

Writers' intentions are the opposite of simple. Firstly, they can vary from writer to writer and work to work. The writer of a satiric or parodic piece must have a conscious intention to satirize or parody, whilst it is highly unlikely that any comparably discrete intention could be associated with the writing of, say, the 'Ode to a Nightingale'. Secondly, writers' intentions are inescapably intertwined with institutional factors: intention is not just what goes on in a writer's head. However original or revolutionary a writer he or she must collaborate or contend with publishing houses, laws (censorship, for instance), educational systems, journal conventions, and so on. And thirdly authorial intentions are multi-layered and in constant process of development. Composition is a *process*. There may be writers whose final drafts are copy-typed from a clear and clean design or plan in the mind, but they must be few and far between if they exist at all. This is why we cannot ever be sure what the final part of Dickens's *The Mystery of Edwin Drood* would have been like had he lived to finish the novel – even though we have various notes of his for the missing section. Like most writers, Dickens in part *discovered* what he wanted to write in the process of writing. (And many writers who, like Dickens, published novels in instalments, were able to modify their plans in line with responses from readers to published early sections, so that with book publication, early instalments might have to be modified to fit later 'intentions'). Joseph Conrad is a writer renowned for starting short stories which grew into long novels – *Lord Jim* and *Under Western Eyes* were both begun as short stories. It is for reasons such as those discussed in this paragraph that it makes sense to say that in some cases a writer's intention is not a design or plan in the author's mind but the work itself. In the course of writing, intentions may crystall-ize which are profoundly at variance with a previously held design or plan: Conrad's plan (outlined in a letter) for *Under Western Eyes* included Razumov's marrying Nathalie Haldin and having a child with her – which does not happen in the published novel. Clearly Wimsatt and Beardsley are quite right that it would be absurd to assume that we can interpret *Under Western Eyes* in the light of this plan.

Authorial revisions present us with a notoriously problematic example of changing intentions. W. H. Auden's alterations to his earlier poems constitute a useful example: many commentators find that these alterations involve so radical a departure from the original spirit of many of the poems that they create a different set of poems; if we take Auden's intention with regard to a single poem over a ten-year period it may include absolutely irreconcilable elements.

Wimsatt and Beardsley allow information concerning a writer's intention which is gathered from the work itself to be acceptable, but we have already noted that the distinction between intrinsic and extrinsic evidence is very hard to sustain in practice. What we find in a work varies according to how we approach it, and how we approach a work is determined by external indicators as well as internal evidence. If we were to rely only on internal evidence of intention then much parody and satire would not be recognizable as such.

Those theorists who have argued about the relevance or other-wise of authorial intention to interpretation have had recourse to two classic 'limit position' arguments: the text produced by natural, non-human agencies, and the author who misinterprets his or her own work. To take the former case (or imagined case) first: if a text were miraculously produced by the action of the sea on a rock, could we read it as a poetic 'object' like any other? Clearly in this case there would be no authorial intention: would this matter? Most readers have felt that it would, and it is doubtless for reasons such as this that F. R. Leavis was so contemptuous of those who could not understand his point that a computer could not possibly write a poem; the concept 'poem' involves a human intention to write a poem. A variant of this argument is the 'accidental meaning' one, and here things start to become a little more complex. According to Frank Cioffi,

> The suspicion that a poetic effect is an accident is fatal to the enjoyment which literature characteristically offers. If the faces on Mount Rushmore were the effect of the action of wind and rain, our relation to them would be very different.[79]

Thus once we know that a particular word in a poem is a misprint, we can no longer go on responding happily to the word, even if we now find the poem with the intended word less satisfactory. And if we know that an author misunderstood the meaning of a word then in reading the work in which that word appears we have problems responding easily to the word.[80] These examples suggest that we are affected in our response to a work of literature both by non-personal standards of usage which are independent of authorial intention and also by our knowledge or estimation of an author's intention.

If this first limit position suggests that authorial intention cannot be discarded or ignored, the second suggests that it is not all-powerful. Frank Cioffi provides a number of relevant examples here – including the following one. Goldsmith was asked what he meant by the word 'slow' in the line from his poem 'The Traveller' which includes the words, 'Remote, unfriended, melancholy, slow'.

> Goldsmith said it meant 'tardiness of locomotion' until contradicted by Johnson. 'No sir. You do not mean tardiness of locomotion. You mean that sluggishness of mind that comes upon a man in solitude.'[81]

What is interesting is that Goldsmith appears to have accepted Johnson's interpretation as correct. Now all that this may mean is that Goldsmith had forgotten what he meant, and if we allow that an author may not be conscious of the creative springs within him or her then again the author could misinterpret his or her own work even while writing it or soon after. In this view literary composition would be purposive but (possibly) partly unconscious: the concept

---

[79]Cioffi, p.68.
[80] A much-quoted example involves Browning's use of the word 'twat' in 'Pippa Passes', believing erroneously that this referred to a form of headgear for nuns, as a result of having misunderstood the lines from *Vanity of Vanities* (1659): 'They talk't of his having a Cardinall's hat; / They'd send him as soon an old Nun's Twat'.
[81] Cioffi, p.67.

of unconscious intention would thus seem to be other than a contradiction in terms. In ordinary usage we tend to assume that intention must be conscious, although it is possible to envisage someone's saying something like, 'I was intending to hurt him, although I was not aware of this at the time.'

E. H. Hirsch has done much in recent years to further debate around the concept of unconscious (literary) intention. According to him we must recognize 'the fundamental distinction between the author's verbal intention and the meanings of which he was explicitly conscious.' The distinction is based on a further distinction between the speaking subject and 'the subjectivity of the author as an actual historical person'; for Hirsch, the speaking subject of a work of literature (not to be confused with a narrator or adopted persona), corresponds 'to a very limited and special aspect of the author's total subjectivity; it is . . . that "part" of the author which specifies or determines verbal meaning.'[82] Hirsch does not altogether escape tautology here, but his central claim is clear: a part of an author's subjectivity can intend meaning without the author as historical individual being conscious of this intention. It could be suggested that this reduces 'intention' to little more than some concept of purposive human direction in verbal utterance.

It is noteworthy that although Hirsch relies upon a model of subjectivity or consciousness which includes separate spheres of direction and determination – 'divided minds' – behind intention he always seems to posit a unitary determining force, even if this is only a 'limited and special aspect of the author's total subjectivity'. But it is possible to see literary works as the product of separate, opposed or warring aspects of an individual's consciousness: the product, indeed, of warring intentions. Moreover, Bakhtin's concern with the dialogic has made us more aware of the problems involved in trying to trace a literary work back to a unitary source.

Let us consider a famous comment on Balzac by Frederick Engels, made in a letter to Margaret Harkness:

> Balzac was politically a legitimist; his great work is a constant elegy on the irretrievable decay of good society; his sympathies are all with the class doomed to extinction. But for all that his satire is never keener, his irony never bitterer than when he sets in motion the very men and women with whom he sympathizes most deeply – the nobles. And the only men of whom he always speaks with undisguised admiration, are his bitterest political antagonists . . . That Balzac thus was compelled to go against his own class sympathies and political prejudices, that he *saw* the necessity of the downfall of his favourite nobles . . . and that he *saw* the real men of the future where, for the time being, they alone were to

---

[82] E. D. Hirsch Jnr., 'Objective Interpretation', repr. in Newton-de Molina, pp. 35, 53.

be found – that I consider one of the greatest triumphs of Realism . . .[83]

The passage provides a model of literary composition which conceives of the writer's artistic insight as something that cuts through his or her consciously held beliefs. The metaphor of visual perception used by Engels consorts rather uneasily with a model which rests on some concept of unitary intention. To 'see' is different from to 'intend'; the former makes of the writer a means whereby truths outside of him or herself can be transmitted to the reader.

Earlier I referred to E. H. Hirsch's distinction between 'meaning' and 'significance', and said that I would return to the problematic issue of a work's meaning. Problematic because, firstly, Hirsch associates meaning exclusively with authorial intention, which we have seen is itself a deeply complex issue; secondly because, as I have also pointed out, it seems reductive to think of a literary work's producing a meaning in the manner that a sentence does: literary works are objects for interpretation, and their reading occasions complex responses. To limit our discussion of literary works to their 'meanings' is to run the risk of cutting out much of what in practice we value them for: 'meaning' is *not* something to which 'interpretation' or 'response' can be reduced. Quentin Skinner has usefully pointed out that when we talk of what a literary work means we may be referring to three different things: 'what do the words mean?'; 'what does this work mean to me?'; and 'what does the writer mean by what he says in this work?'.[84] All three senses can be included in what we mean by 'interpretation' or 'response', or 'appreciation'.

It is arguable that E. D. Hirsch's primary concern is with the issue of authority, and that in pursuing this issue he pays too little attention to the range of uses to which we put literary works. This comes out very clearly in his discussion of the following famous passage from Lewis Carroll's *Through the Looking Glass*.

> 'I don't know what you mean by "glory",' Alice said.
> Humpty Dumpty smiled contemptuously. 'Of course you don't – till I tell you. I meant "there's a nice knock-down argument for you!" '
> 'But "glory" doesn't mean "a nice knock-down argument," ' Alice objected.
> 'When *I* use a word,' Humpty Dumpty said, in rather a scornful tone, 'it means just what I choose it to mean – neither more nor less.'
> 'The question is,' said Alice, 'whether you *can* make words mean so many different things.'
> 'The question is,' said Humpty Dumpty, 'which is to be master – that's all.'

---

[83] Reprinted in many anthologies. The text is actually a draft of a letter sent early 1888.
[84] Skinner, p.212.

Hirsch quotes the last two speeches from this passage at the head of the second chapter of his *Validity in Interpretation*, and his choice of extract is revealing: who is in charge, what is our Court of Appeal? But he omits the earlier part of the passage in which we are shown Humpty Dumpty trying to impose meaning on words in defiance of established convention and usage. In *The Aims of Interpretation* Hirsch quotes the passage in full (at greater length than I have, in fact), and in my opinion gets into the absurd position of trying to defend Humpty Dumpty's right to 'mean' 'there's a nice knock-down argument for you' by saying 'there's glory for you!'

We have Humpty Dumpty's own word for it that such a choice of absolute authority leads to complete solipsism: as Humpty Dumpty tells Alice, she cannot know what he means by a word until he tells her. Were we to follow Hirsch, all verbal communication would involve our first saying a thing and then saying what we meant (and presumably so on *ad infinitum*). Here the protests of the anti-intentionalists seem to carry weight: as Monroe Beardsley points out, what a sentence means depends not on the whim of the individual, and his mental vagaries, 'but upon public conventions of usage that are tied up with habit patterns in the whole speaking community.'[85]

Let us attempt to sum up. Frank Cioffi makes a useful introductory point.

> What any general thesis about the relation of intention to interpretation overlooks is the heterogeneity of the contexts in which questions of interpretation arise. This heterogeneity makes it impossible to give a general answer to the question of what the relevance of intention to interpretation is.[86]

We can add that we do not just interpret works of literature: we respond to, appreciate, study and enjoy them. And the relevance of authorial intention to all of these is not fixed. What we can suggest are some generalized conclusions.

1 The 'conviction that a poet stands in a certain relation to his words conditions our response to them' (Frank Cioffi).[87] Note 'conditions', not 'determines'.
2 'Intention' means different things at different stages of composition: intention is neither necessarily unitary nor is it stable.
3 Conscious and unconscious elements in an author's mind may have a determining effect upon the composition of a literary work and, if known, may affect its reception.
4 An author cannot intend all the implications or effects or

---

[85] Monroe Beardsley, *Aesthetics*, New York, Harcourt, Brace & World, 1958, p.25.
[86] Cioffi, p.58.
[87] Cioffi, p.72.

reception-experiences that his or her work has; to the extent that criticism involves itself with such aspects of the after-life of a literary work then it will make proportionately less sense to seek the sanction of demonstrated authorial intention.

5   Although our conception of 'meaning' may necessarily involve some concept of purposive human agency or direction, an author cannot 'mean' in defiance of all pragmatic and linguistic conventions.

In conclusion, we should perhaps note that when we move from single-author texts to texts with multiple authors, or to the performance arts, then the issue of authorial intention becomes even more complex.

Biographical criticism

The issue of the author's intention or conscious direction of the work does not exhaust the possible need for the critic to take note of the author in criticizing his or her work. Any verbal utterance – spoken or written – may contain elements which call their originator to mind, or elements which can only properly be understood by reference to the character, personality or situation of the person who originated the utterance. T. S. Eliot is associated with the view that poetry should be an escape from personality, and that it is not desirable that poetry should be 'personal'. The demands for literary biography suggest that many readers wish to be able to relate the literary works they read to the works' authors, their lives and experiences. Much could be added to this, but it seems likely that knowledge of the author's biography is one of a number of possible contexts into which the literary work can be fitted and by means of which fitting can be read in slightly different ways. We can choose to read Keats's 'Ode to a Nightingale' with only a very general sense of the author's presence in and behind the poem, or while relating the words more directly to Keats's life and situation at the time of writing. It is of course an error crudely to assume that a line such as 'Where youth grows pale, and spectre-thin, and dies' is 'about Keats's brother Tom', as I saw claimed in a school poetry book once, but it is not illegitimate to allow one's knowledge of Keats's relationship with his brother and the latter's death to enter into one's response to the line.

Author, narrator, persona

Authors rarely speak *in propria persona* in their own works. This is most clear perhaps in the case of drama: none of Shakespeare's plays contain a character named William Shakespeare. But even in poems and novels it is clear that the word 'I' rarely refers unproblematically to the historical author, but rather to a created fictive identity, a fictive subjectivity which may be close to or comparable with that of the historical author, but is not identical with him or her. A single author may use many personae or narrators, and even the 'same' narrator appearing in a number of different works by the same author – Joseph Conrad's Marlow, for instance – is at the reader's peril to be treated as the 'same person'. It is characteristic of untrained or unsophisticated readers that they fail to come to terms with authors' use of personae, and treat statements in literary works as statements made by the author.

An influential concept in this connection is Wayne Booth's 'implied author' – 'an ideal, literary, created version of the real man' which gives us the sense of an intimate relationship with a total and rounded human personality in reading a work. Jane Austen's narrator in *Emma* is not Jane Austen, but it constitutes a sense of a centre of human subjectivity for us while we read the book (even if that sense differs from our sense of a historical individual to the extent that we can refer to 'it' rather than 'him' or 'her').

Alan Sillitoe makes an interesting comment on a related issue in an introduction to a new edition of *Saturday Night and Sunday Morning*. Denying that the novel is autobiographical, Sillitoe nonetheless admits:

> Yet it was in this piece of work that I think I found my true voice, and if I still like it at all, it is for that reason.[88]

The novel is not autobiographical – yet in it Sillitoe found his 'true voice': it is not surprising that we feel that an author's persona is, and is not, 'himself' (or 'herself'). The voice cannot be one used by Sillitoe in his everyday life – otherwise he would not have had to 'find' it; but neither can it be merely that of an invented character, otherwise Sillitoe would hardly describe it as 'my true voice'. Similar comments could be made of the narrative voice in Jane Austen's novels, of Conrad's 'Marlow', and many other personae. It seems that most of us have various voices locked up in us, and that the writer can free one or more of them in the process of composition.

Society, history, culture

It is often assumed that only comparatively recently have critics argued for the necessity of setting a literary work in the context of its author's society and culture, and that such a procedure is one first

[88] Star Book edition, London 1975.

(or mainly) advocated by Marxists. But in his *Preface to Shakespeare* Samuel Johnson made the following comment:

> Every man's performances, to be rightly estimated, must be compared with the state of the age in which he lived, and with his own particular opportunities; and though to the reader a book be not worse or better for the circumstances of the author, yet, as there is always a silent reference of human works to human abilities, and as the enquiry, how far man may extend his designs, or how high he may rate his native force, is of far greater dignity than in what rank we shall place any particular perform-ance, curiosity is always busy to discover the instruments, as well as to survey the workmanship, to know how much is to be ascribed to original powers and how much to casual and adventitious help.

Johnson, to be sure, makes it clear that he is more concerned to assess 'human abilities' than 'human works' – authors rather than texts are his focus of interest here. Nevertheless, his last sentence makes it apparent that he certainly did not assume that a literary work could be seen as the product of an isolated single author. Historical scholarship, he suggests, will enable us to determine what in a work is the product of the individual author, and what the product of the age.

On one level this is straightforward: if we find that a particular image, or verse-form, or narrative technique has been used very frequently by other authors immediately before its use by a particu-lar writer, then we recognize that he or she may have borrowed rather than created it. The matter is more complex than this, however, as even where a writer is most creative and original the presence of social or cultural factors may be detected – either as determining influence or as open or concealed subject matter. As D. H. Lawrence said in his 'Note' to his *Rhyming Poems*,

> It seems to me that no poetry, not even the best, should be judged as if it existed in the absolute. Even the best poetry, when it is at all personal, needs the penumbra of its own time and place and circumstances to make it full and whole . . . What was uttered in the cruel spring of 1917 should not be dislocated and heard as if sounding out of the void.[89]

What Lawrence suggests here is that contextualizing information is needed in order to allow the reader both to understand the literary work as particular speech act made in response to certain circum-stances, and also (perhaps) to limit the reference of the work which, set loose from its genetic context, might be taken to be wider than was intended or is helpful or illuminating.

Lawrence uses the words 'time and place and circumstance'; I have used the words 'society and culture'. This should remind us

[89] Quoted by Holderness, at the start of his book (see note 19).

that *how* we analyse a work's genetic context is very much dependent upon the conceptual tools of analysis at our disposal. A work's
genetic context is not just 'there'; it is reconstructed by means of
analysis using particular concepts and methods; as these develop,
so our understanding of a writer's socio-historical situation can
alter.

Such contextual recreation can provide very different levels of
explanation. On a simple level local associations or references that
have been lost can be rediscovered and made available to readers;
this sort of research is quite closely linked to study of linguistic
change, as it is not just the meanings of individual words that
change but also their connotations, associations, and assumed
reference in a given context. We frequently find that at times when
free political or other comment is dangerous, then concealed
references to political events and figures become more usual, and
are immediately recognized by contemporary readers. (It is
astonishing how many such references to Walpole there are in the
literature of the early eighteenth century in Britain.)

On a slightly higher level, the literary work may have been written as a contribution to a particular debate or controversy, so that
read with no knowledge of this context certain of its features seem
odd. We understand Shelley's *A Defence of Poetry* better when we
realize that it was written in response to Thomas Love Peacock's *The
Four Ages of Poetry*, and E. M. Forster's novel *Howards End* is best
seen in the context of the 'Condition of England' debate. In much
the same way, it helps to know that a literary work was aimed at a
very tightly defined readership, or was published in such a way that
only certain people could have read it.

It is at higher levels than the foregoing that the relating of literary
works to their social and cultural context becomes more complex
and problematic. Complex systems of belief which affected the
writer either consciously or unconsciously, and which can be rediscovered and understood only in terms of the writer's society, have
often been claimed as necessary adjuncts to the full appreciation and
understanding of literary works. Such issues have – especially
recently – often been discussed as part of a general theory of ideologies, and this topic deserves separate consideration at this point.

Ideology

The critic Terry Eagleton has seen the study of ideologies to be the
meta-subject of which Marxist literary criticism forms a part: according to him Marxist literary criticism

> is part of a larger body of theoretical analysis which aims to understand

ideologies – the ideas, values and feelings by which men experience their societies at various times.[90]

Theories of ideology are complex and varied, but central to most of them is the assumption that social, economic and cultural factors do not affect individuals' consciousnesses directly, but in mediated forms. Ideologies are systems of belief and thought, which explain the world to individuals, but which are themselves to be seen in relation to underlying social and historical factors of which the individuals are probably (but in some formulations, not necessarily) unaware. This sounds very much as if ideologies passively reflect particular social situations, but it is additionally argued of them that although they are used to interpret the world and – especially – the social world, they reflect or embody the interests of a particular social class or group. (This last position is by no means one that is universally accepted, and tends to be associated with more traditional Marxist accounts of ideology.) The implications of this position are significant: they involve commitment to a position in some ways similar to that of classical Freudianism. The Freudian sees individuals to be motivated by repressed sexual and other forces which are translated into beliefs and actions not themselves overtly sexual, but embodying sexual forces. In like manner a standard view of ideology sees individuals in the possession of ideologies which reflect particular class interests and by means of which the social world is interpreted. In both cases the individual is unaware (or may be unaware) of the true forces determining his or her world-view. It should be added that (again in a traditional Marxist account), the class interests or position that a person's ideology reflects may not be those of the person's own class, but of (in a typical formulation) a separate ruling class.

A possible example of such an ideological displacement would be that of religion: the individual not only believing in certain things, but believing that he or she holds these beliefs because they are true, while actually (the argument runs) holding them because they reflect the class interests of a ruling class which uses such beliefs (again, probably unconsciously) to guarantee a particular interpretation of the world and thus forms of behaviour which are in the interests of that ruling class.

A classic application of such a view of ideology to literature is Lucien Goldmann's book *The Hidden God*. According to Goldmann any great literary or artistic work is the expression of a world vision which is the product of a collective group consciousness which reaches its highest expression in the mind of a poet or thinker.

[90] Terry Eagleton, *Marxism and Literary Criticism*, London, Methuen, 1976, p.viii.

Goldmann does not himself share the belief that this world vision represents the interests of another class, but argues that it expresses a group's social and historical situation. Thus the world vision expressed in its highest affirmation by individuals such as Racine and Pascal represents the tragic social and historical situation of the French *noblesse de robe* to which these individuals felt an allegiance. To understand and appreciate the plays of Racine, therefore, one needs to set them in the context of that particular social group's historical situation – something to which the plays do not draw overt attention. Many parallel forms of literary interpretation or understanding could be suggested. Critics quite unconnected with Marxism have argued that the portrayal of God and Satan in Milton's 'Paradise Lost' can only be understood in the light of Milton's own experience as a republican rebel against the absolute power of a hereditary monarch. Many nineteenth-century novels end with the reconciliation of personal antagonisms between individual workers and capitalists which indicate a desire for such reconciliation on a larger scale.

What problems are there with the use of such concepts of ideology to understand and explain literary works?

Firstly, the problem that all theories of hidden determinants or reflections are faced with: that of demonstrating that there actually is a determining link between the posited determining factor and the literary work. By its very nature a theory of ideological influence involves a complex and indirect process of mediation. Such processes are notoriously difficult to establish beyond reasonable doubt. It seems to be the case that the more general the link argued the less such problems appear, but trying to explain a particular detail in a literary work by reference to a writer's ideology is often far more problematic.

A second problem is that there is a strong case to be made that the greatest writers are precisely those who rise above the ideological assumptions of the mass of their fellows, and see through to those underlying realities concealed and distorted in the ideology in question. ('See through' in the sense of artistically penetrate rather than consciously perceive.) Even Goldmann admits that Pascal was too rigorous and exact a thinker to accept the ideology of the society in which he lived in a purely passive manner.[91] It has been argued of a number of writers that their artistic vision is at odds with and superior to their consciously held beliefs (Dickens is one obvious example).

Associated with this problem we can raise the issue of the extent to which ideologies are consistent systems, or collections of more or

[91] Lucien Goldmann, *The Hidden God*, London, Routledge, 1964, p.304.

less inconsistent beliefs and assumptions held together by a combination of habit and social indoctrination. Louis Althusser has argued that an ideology is internally unified by a particular problematic,[92] but it is possible to claim the opposite, that it is precisely because ideologies are not consciously held as ideologies that problems of internal consistency may be altogether ignored.

It is worth noting, in conclusion, that it is not just writers and literary works, but also critics and critical theories which may be susceptible to being interpreted in terms of their reflecting, in a concealed manner, their social situation. Thus Frank Lentricchia remarks ironically of the 'American Derridean', that his or her desire to experience the joy of freedom may be seen as

> a reflection (and tacit acknowledgment) . . . of a situation in which that kind of freedom is denied all round, a situation in which oppression, not freedom, characterizes social existence.[93]

(It could, alternatively, be seen as a reflection of his or her social and political isolation and powerlessness, a situation in which 'playing with texts' is all that he or she feels able in practice to do.)

If one way of exploring the link between literature and its socio-historical genesis is in terms of the influence of ideas, situations and events on *what* is written, another is through concern with *how* writing is supported, disseminated and received – a concern which in time may well in part determine what is written. This topic requires consideration in a separate section.

The sociology of literature

Writers have to live. They need either to be born to wealth, or to be provided with the means to live in one or more of a variety of ways. They can have a rich patron, they can receive subscriptions for their work, they can sell the copyright of their work to a publisher, they can receive a wage from a publisher, or they can receive royalties from the sales of their books. Or they can write alongside another job which provides them with a living income. Literature also – obviously – requires readers. Readers have to be literate. In some societies most adults are literate – in others few are. Sometimes women constitute the bulk of a particular reading group, in other circumstances most women may be illiterate. Literature may be freely available to all in public libraries, or it may be available only in books too expensive to be purchased by most people. A society may have no restrictive rules about what literature may be published, or

---

[92] Louis Althusser, *For Marx*, trans. Ben Brewster, London, Allen Lane, 1969, p.62.
[93] Frank Lentricchia, *After the New Criticism*, London, Methuen, 1983, p.182.

it may exercise heavy censorship.

These are the sorts of issues looked at by sociologists of literature. Clearly they can all have an effect on the sort of literary works that are written, and on what these literary works contain. To this extent it may well be dangerous to follow E. M. Forster's advice (in *Aspects of the Novel*) and to envisage the novelists of history all writing their novels at once, all at work in a circular room, and believing that 'the feel of the pen between their fingers' is more important than the fall of empires outside this room. Forster's friend Virginia Woolf was, in contrast, sure that her inheritance of £500 a year was crucial to the development of her art as a novelist;[94] she knew that to be conscious only of the feel of the pen between one's fingers one needs to be confident about the meal that awaits one when one has finished writing that day, and the reader who awaits when the book is finished.

We cannot understand Shakespeare's art fully if we are not aware of the composition of his audience, nor can we appreciate the turns of plot in Dickens's *Martin Chuzzlewit* if we are unaware of the fact that some of these occurred because Dickens responded to low sales in early instalments by deciding to send Martin to America.

[94] See *A Room of One's Own*.

V

Reference and Fictionality

The question of what – if anything – literary works refer to is one that has exercized critics since antiquity. In a relatively crude version of the debate this has involved accusing writers of lying: in the sixth century BC the Athenian legislator Solon complained of the many lies told by poets, and his charge has been rehearsed by many subsequent commentators. Joseph Conrad, for example, was fond of playing on the double meaning of the word 'fiction', and on one occasion regretted the fact that he 'never could invent an effective lie – a lie that would sell, and last, and be admirable.' But Conrad also wrote that at the heart of fiction, 'even the least worthy of the name, some sort of truth can be found', and he further claimed that fiction was nearer truth than history, 'being based on the reality of forms and the observation of social phenomena, whereas history is based on documents, and the reading of print and handwriting – on second-hand impression.'[95]

Writers are accused of telling lies, then, yet their accusers are not above admitting that their works contain some form of truth. On such apparently paradoxical assertions centuries of debate have flourished.

Yet it is not hard to see what lies behind the paradox. Writers describe characters, events, actions which have never existed out-side the pages of their work; they also attribute statements and actions to historical personages about which they could not know had they a historical reality. On the other hand, literary works have been studied and respected for centuries as the source of wisdom and insight. Scientists (including both Freud and Marx) have had repeated recourse to literature as a source of understanding of the world, and the education systems of developed countries (and many developing countries) throughout the world make the study of literature compulsory.

[95] (i) Letter to R. B. Cunninghame Graham May 1898, in C. T. Watts (ed.), *Joseph Conrad's Letters to R. B. Cunninghame Graham*, London, Cambridge UP, 1969, p.85; (ii) 'Books' (1905), in *Notes on Life and Letters*, Dent Collected Edition, p.6; (iii) 'Henry James: An Appreciation', in *Notes on Life and Letters*, p.17.

One renowned attempt to resolve this paradox was made by Sir Philip Sidney in his *An Apology for Poetry* (1595). Sidney sets out to answer the accusation that poets are liars, and argues:

> Now, for the poet, he nothing affirms, and so therefore never lieth.
>
> . . .
>
> And therefore, though he recount things not true, yet because he telleth them not for true, he lieth not . . .

Presumably Sidney might have been disturbed by the duplicity of Daniel Defoe, who passed novels such as *Moll Flanders* off as factual accounts; leaving such examples aside, however, Sidney's defence may excuse writers of the charge of lying, but at a price many commentators have found too high. For if the writer affirms nothing, then it would appear to follow that the literary work has nothing to say about the world or the people in it. Sidney's position has, nonetheless, its modern defenders. Elder Olson has argued that poetic statements

> must not be confused . . . with propositions; since they are not statements about things which exist outside the poem, it would be meaningless to evalutate them as true or false . . .[96]

Is this true? Consider the following poem by John Keats:

> The House of Mourning written by Mr. Scott, –
>   A sermon at the Magdalen, – a tear
>   Dropt on a greasy novel, – want of cheer
> After a walk up hill to a friend's cot, –
> Tea with a Maiden Lady – a curs'd lot
>   Of worthy poems with the Author near, –
>   A patron lord – a drunkenness from beer, –
> Haydon's great picture, – a cold coffee pot
> At midnight when the muse is ripe for labour, –
>   The voice of Mr. Coleridge, – a french Bonnet
> Before you in the pit, – a pipe & tabour, –
> A damn'd inseparable flute and neighbour,–
>   All these are vile, – But viler Wordsworth's Sonnet
>   On Dover:- Dover! – who *could* write upon it?

Surely to make any sense at all of this poem one has to understand that the long list of things called vile in the poem refers to entities outside, not inside, the world of the poem. How could we understand the poem in any way were this not so? And this applies both to

[96] Elder Olson,' 'Sailing to Byzantium'': Prolegomena to a Poetics of the Lyric'. Repr. in W. S. Scott (ed.), *Five Approaches of Literary Criticism*, London, Collier–Macmillan, 1962, p.226.

the specific references to real people and places and also to the generalized experiences. If it were the case that the statements in the poem were not about things outside the poem we could hardly be amused by the poem. (I might add that when, on Christmas Day 1970, I was stranded in the town of Dover, I recalled Keats's poem with a grim satisfaction.)

It would, I suppose, be possible to argue that the statements in Keats's poem are not 'poetic statements', but this would be to fly in the face of accepted usage. Obviously literary works contain a range of different sorts of statement: even within this poem we can detect what is probably humorous exaggeration (Coleridge's voice), direct statement about an actual literary work (*The House of Mourning*), ironic hinting (Haydon's 'great' picture – in size or worth?), and non-specific references to classes of experience. But to deny that some or all of these were properly poetic statements would be to impoverish our concept of poetry. And to say that Keats's poem presents us with exaggeration is not to say that it does not refer to what it exaggerates about; to exaggerate about something necessarily involves making a proposition about it.

It is a historical irony, perhaps, that just when the view that literature was non-referential was becoming distinctly unfashionable, an extremely fashionable set of critical beliefs brought this belief back into favour. Structuralism and Post-structuralism have once more made it theoretically respectable to make statements such as the following:

> literature (by being non-referential) makes us aware of the true (i.e. Saussurean) nature of language.[97]

Along with Saussure, the Russian and Czech Formalists have lent weight to the argument that literature is non-referential; Jan Mukařovský, for example, claimed that, 'the question of truthfulness does not apply in regard to the subject matter of a work of poetry.'[98] But it is Saussurean linguistics (which, as I have pointed out, may wander a long way from what Saussure ever believed) that has provided the main theoretical justification for this position. It is claimed, for example, that just as a word (signifier) such as 'tree' does not refer to a real, living tree but to the concept of a tree, so too does literature not refer to things in the world but either to itself or to other texts or, at best, concepts.

> it was [Saussure's] idea of the arbitrary and differential nature of the sign, and therefore of the essential disjunction between language and

[97] Ann Jefferson, 'Structuralism and Post-structuralism', in Jefferson and Robey, p.86.
[98] Mukařovský, p.22.

reality, that became the foundation of the structuralist movement. It was from this starting-point that the structuralists arrived at the radical view that all meaning in every sphere of human activity consists of closed systems wholly independent of the material world.[99]

If language cannot refer to the material world, we have to assume that the phrase 'the material world' in the above quotation does not actually refer to the material world, but to the concept of the material world. What Saussurean linguistics seems to have no theory of is where our concepts come from; if they are locked within wholly closed meaning systems then it is certainly not from the material world. We must thus have a concept of the material world which has arisen independently of, and does not refer to, the material world. The title of Fredric Jameson's book on structuralism – *The Prison-house of Language* – is well-chosen.

Clearly such a theoretical position is riddled with problems. Why do changes/variations in language seem to correlate with variations in the material world and varying human responses to it? (Can a Structuralist explain why the Eskimaux have so many words in their language for types of snow? Is it because there are lots of snow-concepts drifting around in Canada?)

Some readers may be finding this whole discussion a little irritating: what do such abstract issues have to do with the reading of literature? Well, questions about whether particular literary works either refer to ordinary, non-literary things, events, and experiences (and if so *how*), or require that the reader possess knowledge of such things, events and experiences, recur surprisingly frequently. I will come back to some of the issues involved, in my discussion of realism later on in this section. At this point I will merely stress that certain philosophical positions *vis-à-vis* literary works' referentiality or otherwise have profound implications for our view of literature. (Do we, for example, escape out of reality into the closed world of a literary work, or does the literary work alter our view of and involvement in the extra-literary world? Do we read about reality, or life, in a literary work – or take refuge from them in it? Are our normal opinions about and knowledge of reality essential to a reading of a literary work? Or are they comparable to our domestic currency when we travel abroad: valueless, or valueless unless changed into something else?)

A more general problem facing all non-referential theories of literature relates to the issues of censorship and control of literature by governments and their organs. If literature is a closed realm, neither referring to the world nor affecting behaviour in it (I shall come on to the latter view in due course), then why should anyone

[99] David Robey, p.43.

ever want to change or suppress literary works? Because people insist on reading them in a non-literary manner? This seems such a weak position that I shall not pursue it. I will only add that from a Structuralist point of view it is presumably impossible for a literary work (or anything else) to libel a person. And when we move to the Deconstructionist position that 'there is nothing outside the text',[100] then we seem to be left with nothing for literature to libel or refer to.

Let us return to a more detailed consideration of what variety of forms of statement can be found in literary works. *Can* a literary work contain lies? On a non-problematic level, of course, a character in a novel can be represented as telling lies to another. Less trivially, a literary work may contain general or particular statements which appear to have authorial sanction (they are not uttered, for example, by an 'unreliable narrator'), but which are not true. This description seems straightforward, but it actually covers a range of possible alternatives. Such statements can be equivalent to 'Let us imagine that "X" is true' given the conventions governing literary discourse in a given culture; the words 'Once upon a time there was . . .' are the conventional means whereby a writer of a particular sort of story asks his or her readers to imagine a described state of affairs. Again, the author may believe the statements to be true, although actually they are not. Or, finally, the author may know the statements to be false, and may wish to mislead the reader into believing them. It is conceivable, for example, that Coleridge actually had a very pleasant voice, that Keats knew this to be the case, but out of spite wrote a poem that he thought would mislead future generations. In that case it seems clear to me that Keats would have been lying. And the same could be said where the falsehood was made – deliberately – through insinuation or hint. Borderline cases occur when a work is represented – or represents itself – as bearing a very close relationship to a particular set of facts in the extra-literary world, but where a detail – or several – has been consciously changed. This can be part of the shaping of a literary work from the raw material of experience (it is a very common situation), but it could be done deliberately for malicious reasons.

A more common problem is that of the work which contains what appear to be references to the outside world which are not literally accurate. We would not expect a historian to go to Tolstoy's *War and Peace* as primary material for a history of the Franco–Russian war – or, for that matter, to *St. Joan* for a biography of the saint. On the other hand, we would surely feel uneasy to be told that it would ideally be better were readers of *War and Peace* to know nothing of

[100] Jacques Derrida's much-quoted statement, 'Il n'y a pas de hors texte' suggests both that there is nothing outside the text and also that there is no 'outer text'.

this war, and that those unfortunate enough to be possessed of some such knowledge should expel it from their consciousness. Moreover, if *no* other material existed, it would be legitimate for a historian of the war in question to use Tolstoy's novel – just as historians of much older wars have had to rely on or have recourse to evidence in literary works. Tolstoy could easily have set his novel in an imagined country peopled by imaginary characters only; that he set it in Russia and included a character called Napoleon can be said to indicate that he wished to utilize his readers' knowledge of the historical Russia and the historical Napoleon (which is not to say that there is no difference between the historical and the fictional Napoleon).

A distinction that is much referred to in discussions such as this is that of Gottlob Frege's between *Sinn* and *Bedeutung* – usually translated as sense (or meaning), and reference. Frege points out that phrases such as 'The Morning Star' and 'The Evening Star' have the same reference (the planet Venus), but a different sense (the planet seen in the morning or seen in the evening, with varied cultural and literary connotations). Certain literary theorists have attempted to use this distinction to get at the peculiar form of truth or reference that they see inhering in literary works. Thus they might argue that the reference of 'Napoleon' in Tolstoy's novel is the historical French general, but that the sense or meaning of this word in its literary context is different, that certain entailments are deleted by the literary context and others are – in the course of the narrative's development – added.

It seems important to establish that literary works can involve different sorts and degrees of reference to extra-literary reality, and that a range of such levels of reference can co-exist in the same work – even in the same literary utterance. Some literary works seem to me to rest so close to non-literary utterances in the matter of reference that it is more or less impossible to distinguish the two. In certain cases it seems to me that the voice of the author speaks directly through a literary work – in the lyric poetry of Sorley Maclean, for example, or many of the more recent poems of Seamus Heaney. This is *not* to say that such poems are identical with non-poetic utterances, but merely to say that their literariness or poeticality does not reside in a unique form of referentiality, or in their use of a literary persona.

At one remove from such examples are literary works which seem to me to make statements about the world, but on the basis of statements which, were they to have been made in non-literary contexts, would have been termed lies. To put it another way: we are not too bothered whether the historical Wordsworth really did meet an old man upon the moor and utter exactly the words he places in the mouth of his poetic persona in 'Resolution and Independence'; the conventions of poetry – unlike those of, for example, police investigations or accounts to one's spouse explaining why one is late home – do not demand that sort of referential accuracy. Moreover, even were we to learn that Wordsworth most definitely did not ever utter such words, this would still not prevent us from believing that his poem makes reference to problems and issues that are not just literary, but are those of the real world in which Wordsworth lived and which exercised him personally:

> Cold, pain and labour, and all fleshly ills;
> And mighty poets in their misery dead.

These physical ills are not poetic constructs: they are, surely, what they always have been in the everyday world, and the 'mighty poets' are not fictional characters but actual individuals who can be identified from the information given in the poem.

At this stage it may be useful to introduce a crude distinction between particular and general reference – which I touched upon when talking of Keats's sonnet. A writer can choose to invent, or to distort particular facts, in a literary work, so as to make assertions about the extra-literary world which have a generalizing truth. Joseph Conrad makes this point rather well in a letter to a friend:

> As you know, I do not write history, but fiction and I am therefore entitled to choose as I please what is most suitable in regard to characters and particulars to help me in the general impression I wish to produce.[101]

Much later, Conrad wrote in another letter to Richard Curle, who was to write about a new edition of Conrad's works,

> Suppose you opened by a couple of short paragraphs of general observation on authors and their material, how they transform it from particular to general, and appeal to universal emotions by the temperamental handling of personal experience?[102]

I have mentioned earlier Conrad's habit of playing with the double meaning of the word 'fiction' in English, and it seems probable that a sense that 'truth' and 'fiction' are not synonymous is a factor in beliefs concerning the 'lying' of authors. But it is not hard to demonstrate that literary fiction and lying are, in essence, very different

---

[101] G. Jean-Aubry, *Joseph Conrad Life and Letters*, London, Heinemann, 1927, vol. 1, p.77.
[102] Richard Curle (ed.), *Conrad to a Friend*, London, Sampson Low, Marston, 1928, p.195.

things. Jonathan Swift was reportedly much amused by the account of an Irish bishop who had read *Gulliver's Travels* and reported that it was full of impenetrable lies and that for his part he hardly believed a word of it. The good bishop's response – like Huckleberry Finn's response to the circus performance – is an example of a failure to perceive the nature of the work he comments on, and it shows that there is a major difference between recognizing that a book is not literally true and that it is a work of literary fiction.

It seems to be the case that in our society we are socialized into an understanding of fiction, and that playing with toys, 'make-believe', jokes and story-telling are some of the activities which effect this socialization alongside actual schooling in the reading of fiction. As Thomas Pavel remarks, literary texts, 'like most informal collections of sentences . . . display a property that may puzzle logicians but that doubtless appears natural to anyone else: their truth as a whole is not recursively definable starting from the truth of the individual sentences that constitute them.'[103]

Fiction is a significant component in our normal, everyday lives: we get up, look at the comic strip in the daily newspaper, read a novel on the bus into work, share jokes with our work-mates, come home and play games with our children, and then switch the television on and watch a soap-opera on TV. All of these activities involve the mental manipulation of fictional constructs according to certain rules and conventions, none of them present the vast majority of adults with any problems (we are not even conscious of doing anything special when we engage in them) – and yet on analysis they turn out to involve enormously complex mediations between fiction and reality. A good demonstration of this is given by Thomas C. Schelling in an analysis of peoples' responses to the 'death' of Lassie on television. He points out that with very few exceptions those millions of viewers who grieved at Lassie's death knew that not only did 'Lassie' not exist but also that the real dog who represented her was alive and well. He adds that viewers would not be satisfied by an added, alternative episode depicting Lassie as alive and well, and prefaced with the statement that as she was only fictional, and as her death upset so many, this alternative story-ending had been produced. On the other hand, were it to be proved that the regular script-writer had been hospitalized, and that a substitute writer had written Lassie's 'death', then viewers might accept a replacement episode.[104] (For the same reason continuations of unfinished novels such as Dickens's *Edwin Drood* by other writers

[103] Pavel, p.17.
[104] Thomas C. Schelling, 'The Mind as Consuming Organ', in Jon Elster (ed.), *The Multiple Self*, London, Cambridge UP, 1985, p.177.

are never really satisfactory – and readers of Avellaneda's unauthorized continuation of Cervantes's *Don Quixote* had no difficulty in rejecting it as inauthentic.) It would seem that at this level there is some justice in the claim of the Structuralists that our unconscious awareness of certain literary rules and conventions is comparable to our unconscious awareness of the rules of grammar. And just as the formal study of language attempts to transfer these implicitly understood rules of grammar into a formal, written grammar, so the formal study of literature attempts (among other things) to bring to the surface the rules of literary response.

Our ability to 'immerse' ourselves in fiction, to live in the 'world' of a literary work, is a fascinating and complicated procedure – familiar to us yet, when observed dispassionately, extraordinary. Bakhtin points out that not all literary genres offer this form of involvement: we can enter the world of the novel but not that of the epic, for example. And even in such experiences, as Samuel Johnson pointed out when rejecting the doctrine of the unities,[105] we never lose a sense of the art-work as art-work and not reality itself. As Barbara Herrnstein Smith puts it, 'The illusions of art are never *de*lusions. The artwork interests, impresses, and moves us both as the thing represented and as the *representing* itself.'[106]

Certain things follow from what I have said concerning the nature of fictional experiences. Firstly, that in discussing a literary work such as a novel we have a choice between discussing it as crafted production and as lived experience for the reader. (Most critics actually oscillate between the two alternatives.) And secondly, that to be able to read fiction in a more sophisticated way than Swift's Irish bishop is not necessarily to be prepared to accept that no mirroring or depiction of the external world occurs in a literary work. To realize that the particulars of a literary work are not literally true, that the work has no simplistic or mechanistic relationship to extra-textual reality, is not necessarily to accept that the work contains no reference to the non-literary world – although a number of critics have assumed that this is the case.

If a literary work relies upon the reader's bringing certain knowledge from the world in order to understand the work, then literary works cannot be said to be unconnected to the non-literary world. 'Bringing knowledge to' and 'referring' are often two ways of saying the same thing: if *Howards End* relies upon its readers' understanding of what a motor-car is, then the novel refers to motor-cars (and this is true even if motor-cars in the novel are given qualities which

[105]See Johnson's *Preface* to his edition of Shakespeare.
[106] Barbara Herrnstein Smith, 'Poetry as Fiction', in Ralph Cohen (ed.), *New Directions in Literary History*, London, Routledge, 1974, 187.

they do not have in the real world). Some works of literature impel the reader to discover relatively specialist knowledge in order to be fully appreciated. To understand Joseph Conrad's *The Secret Sharer* and *Typhoon* one really needs to know whether the nautical decisions of the respective captains were deemed to constitute good or bad seamanship at the time that Conrad wrote.

What, however, of the argument that the successful work provides us with all the knowledge that we need to appreciate it? Well, in practice, surely no work does this fully: all require that we bring a knowledge of a language with us in our reading, and to know a language is to know a culture and a part of the world.

We should also remember that *representation* is central to literary reference, and that representation never works on a simple one-to-one basis: it is either partial, taking the part for the whole, or involves more complex coding processes such as the condensation and displacement Freud traced in dream representation. It is for this reason that a single item in a piece of representation may involve reference on a range of different levels. Where representation is partial it has involved choice, and thus is in part a commentary on the reality it selectively imitates.

Realism

We are now nibbling at the edges of the complex topic of realism. I will leave aside discussion of the use of this term to describe a particular school or set of conventions, and will concentrate upon the problematic theoretical issues the term raises.

Discussion of realism by literary theorists has been heavily influenced by Marxism, but by no means all who argue for literary realism are Marxists.

Central to the debates about literary realism is a concern with certain key philosophical issues concerning the relationship between mind and world. As Terry Lovell puts it,

> Modern epistemological realism accepts much of the conventionalist critique of empiricism. In particular, it concedes that knowledge is socially constructed and that language, even the language of experience, is theory-impregnated. Yet it retains the empiricist insistence that the real world cannot be reduced to language or to theory, but is independent of both, and yet knowable.[107]

The contrast with what I earlier presented as the Saussurean view of language (attributed to rather than claimed by Saussure), should be obvious. The world exists independent of language and theory,

[107] Terry Lovell, *Pictures of Reality*, London, BFI, 1980, p.17.

even if these are – in part at least – our means of getting to know the world.

We can refer to these two ways of picturing the mind–world relationship as idealist and realist, and they obviously have important implications both for writers and for critics and theorists. A striking feature of literary works produced in the Western world during the present century is that they seem generally susceptible to being divided between these two philosophical positions. What is known as modernist literature often seems to posit the existence of a set of multiple and irreconcilable realities, realities produced by different individuals living in worlds of their own creation. Realist literature, in contrast, posits a single world – it is monist rather than pluralist *vis-à-vis* reality – which may be conceived partially and in different ways by different individuals and in different contexts, but which is essentially independent of such perceptions.

Now such a division is crude, leaves a number of unanswered problems, and has to be applied with great caution. (James Joyce, for example, is undoubtedly a modernist, but many – myself included – would argue that he is also a realist in philosophical terms.) But in spite of such problems, the distinction is useful, and clearly has important implications for criticism. Because both views posit a completely different view of the relationship between mind and world they involve a different conception of the relationship between the work and the world. We can thus relate so-called Saussurean linguistics, literary-critical formalism, and modernism to an essentially idealist set of assumptions, while realist literature and – say – Marxist literary criticism would share an opposing set. But in both cases the views of the critic would condition his or her approach to the analysis of a given literary work, irrespective of the philosophy discoverable in the work or attributable to its author.

According to most standard doctrines of literary realism all literary works in some way reflect extra-literary reality, but they can do so fragmentarily, chaotically, and in a manner that makes it impossible for the reader better to understand the world from a perusal of the work, or, alternatively, they can reflect extra-literary reality self-consciously and with due attention to the whole of reality, so that the reader can use the work as a means of learning about the world.

This is the burden, at any rate, of Georg Lukács's long-running defence of realism and attack on modernist literature and art. According to Lukács, 'every major realist' has as goal the penetration of the laws governing objective reality, and the uncovering of 'the deeper, hidden, mediated, not immediately perceptible network of relationships that go to make up society'.[108]

[108] Ernst Bloch *et al*, *Aesthetics and Politics*, London, NLB, 1977, p.38.

In recent years we have been able to read the comments of Bertholt Brecht on Lukács's views, and the two sides of this dispute have become known as the Brecht–Lukács debate. For Lukács, 'realist' was an honorific term: to say that Thomas Mann, Balzac, Dickens and Tolstoy were realists was to state that each 'knows how thoughts and feelings grow out of the life of society and how experiences and emotions are parts of the total complex of reality.' Moreover, each, according to Lukács, 'as a realist . . . assigns these parts to their rightful place within the total life context', showing 'what area of society they arise from and where they are going to.'[109]

One immediate point worth making about such a formulation is that it seems difficult to imagine how it might be applied to lyric poetry; Lukács's concentration upon the novel allows him to avoid some awkward questions. A second point is that Lukács's position is in some ways curiously *textual*; by this I mean that realism is limited to a question of what is in texts, and is less a question of how texts are read or criticized. And further, that the text must in some way involve the whole of a particular reality – all of a given society, a 'total life context'.

Now in contrast to this Brecht's starting-point is actually wider, for he involves not just the text or the literary work in his discussion but also a view of the particular set of relationships amongst the components of the literary process at a given time and place. The text is seen not just in relation to a 'total life context', but in the context of particular struggles involving specific audiences, conditions of reception, relationships with other aspects of life, and so on. As he says,

> Even the realistic mode of writing, of which literature provides many very different examples, bears the stamp of the way it was employed, when and by which class, down to its smallest details. With the people struggling and changing reality before our eyes, we must not cling to 'tried' rules of narrative, venerable literary models, eternal aesthetic laws. We must not derive realism as such from particular existing works, but we shall use every means, old and new, tried and untried, derived from art and derived from other sources, to render reality to men in a form they can master.[110]

Whereas Lukács's emphasis is on the text's including a model of a given social totality, Brecht's is on the text as one component in a struggle involving many different aspects, a text that has to be seen not in itself but in the context of this total struggle and of the particular relationships between the components of the literary process.

[109] Bloch, p.36.
[110] Bloch, p.81.

Brecht's insistence that 'reality changes; in order to represent it, modes of representation must also change',[111] highlights a problem of the theory of realism that many have accused Lukács of ignoring. The world and the work are linked by complex chains of representational codes and conventions which change from age to age. Thus works or aspects of works are not realistic in themselves, but when interpreted in the light of the appropriate codes and conventions.

Now this has led some to see the issue of realism as something internal to interpretative conventions. In his essay 'On Realism in Art', Roman Jakobson notes that works of art may be called realistic either if the author intends them as such, or if the perceiver interprets them as true to life. He then notes that the author who wishes to create a realistic work will modify artistic conventions so as to strike the perceiver with the unexpected and force him or her to look at reality with fresh eyes. Realism thus involves constant deformation of formulae or ideograms in the interests of 'making new'.[112]

As I have suggested, such a model is highly 'internal' in its view of realism. Conventions, codes of representation, become stale and clichéd – the artist wishing to make people see reality afresh must constantly deform those conventions and codes. It is in such a manner that the Russian Formalist advocacy of 'defamiliarization' is explained. But Brecht is surely right to imply that the creation and replacement of artistic conventions is by no means a purely internal, 'artistic' issue. It is conditioned by changes in audiences and in the economics of writing, by the opening of writing and reading to new social groups, by alterations in other art-forms, by public events and by anything that can change a people's or a group's consciousness.

Lukács, then, sees realism as largely a question of the text's depiction of a social totality; Jakobson sees it as the manipulation of artistic conventions so as to make the perceivers of art-works see reality with a fresh eye; but Brecht sees it to involve both the relationship between the art-work and society (an active relationship, not the passive view of a detached observer for Brecht), and also the complex way in which an art-work is used by its perceivers as part of a larger struggle, within which the issue of artistic conventions is by no means negligible. Brecht shifts the focus of discussion from the question, 'Is this work realistic?', to the question, 'Does this work at this particular time and in this context lead us to perceive reality in a broader, more appropriate, more revealing way?'

Interestingly, Brecht does *not* want his readers to sink into the world of the work and to forget the real world outside: for him

---

[111] Bloch, p.82.
[112] Jakobson, p.38.

realism involves constantly drawing the audience's attention to the fact that the art-work is an art-work, and different from reality. As Brecht argues, 'odd as it may seem, the mere reproduction of reality does not give an impression of truth.'[113] Putting it another way, we can say that the events, situations or characters in a literary work do not have to be *like* the real world to make us *think about it*:[114] satire and parody classically involve distortion and exaggeration, yet they do direct our attention to the extra-literary world. The point is perhaps well summed up by a couple of comments Joseph Conrad made in letters. Writing to Arnold Bennett he commented:

> I would quarrel not with the truth of your conception but with the realism thereof. You stop just short of being absolutely real because you are faithful to your dogmas of realism. Now realism in art will never approach reality.[115]

And in a letter to H. G. Wells he refers to Wells as a 'Realist of the Fantastic!'.[116]

Self-reference/reflexivity

The 'defamiliarization' of the Russian Formalists – like Brecht's 'Alienation effect' – not only involves the disruption of normal perceptual habits so as to induce a new view of reality; it also involves the production of texts which draw attention to themselves as texts, which refer to themselves. Some commentaries on literary self-reference suggest that this is a comparatively recent phenomenon, and it is certainly true that much modernist literature is distinguished by its 'self-consciousness', a form of awareness produced by textual self-reference among other things. But there is a tradition of literary self-reference that dates back long before the present century. Indeed, almost any example of parody or satire, any sudden breaking of the literary rules or flouting of convention, necessarily has the effect of drawing attention to the text as text. The introduction of the players in *Hamlet*, and the discussion which their performance generates, also remind the audience that they too are watching players: such concealed forms of self-reference (of which Shakespeare's plays are full) can hardly be limited to the modern period. Many lyric poets refer to the poem as poem in the poem, and *Tristram Shandy* is by no means the only or earliest example of

---

[113] John Willett, (ed. and trans.), *Brecht on Theatre*, London, Methuen, repr. 1974, p.11.
[114] For an interesting discussion of some of these issues, see John O. Thompson, 'Up Aporia Creek', in *Screen Education* 31, Summer 1979, p.29 ff.
[115] Jean-Aubry, p.303.
[116] Jean-Aubry, p.259.

extensive fictional self-reference.

More overt forms of self-reference raise a number of interesting theoretical questions. In particular, they force us to ask whether different literary works require awareness of the text as text as part of the actual reading experience, whereas others require immersion in the world of the work during the reading experience, but consideration of it as work on completion of reading. Such continual oscillation between immersion in and consciousness of the text during reading may arguably serve the aims of realism, inasmuch as the reader is continually forced to compare and contrast the world and the work – rather than experiencing the work as a world closed in itself and of a different level of reality from the extra-literary world. Literary self-reference may also force a more active form of reading on the reader, as he or she has to struggle to establish how and why the text requires to be perceived in different ways – as window on the world and window in the world, or as world or work. In one sense techniques of literary self-reference force the reader into dialogue with the author and work.

It is perhaps interesting how we have proceeded from a discussion of the way in which the text reflects or depicts an external reality to a consideration of the manner whereby literary texts work on their readers and effect changes in their view of reality. *Realism*, then, is not just a question of what is 'in' literary works, but of what these do to their readers.

Intertextuality and transtextuality

In one of the 'Pink Panther' films Inspector Clouseau – played by Peter Sellers – casually spins a large globe while engaged in conversation, then, forgetting what he has done, leans on the spinning globe and is thrown across the room by it. In a subsequent film in the same series the same situation is set up, except that at the last moment instead of being thrown across the room the Inspector has his fingers painfully jammed between the revolving globe and its frame.

The pleasure audiences get from the second scene includes a certain reference to the earlier one. As the second scene is prepared those who have seen the first typically feel a sense of disappointment and resentment that the same joke is being repeated, only to find that the director has been playing with them, and having led them to expect one turn of events has given them a different one. In one sense, then, the second scene refers to the first: not overtly, but nonetheless clearly.

This trivial example can serve as a basic model for the enormously complex links and relationships between different literary works. In a sense, any generic expectation involves a reference of one literary work to others, and to establish a tradition is to establish relations between a number of different literary works. Intertextuality can either be very specific – as in the Pink Panther example – or it can involve diffuse and highly mediated patterns of influence and reference. According to T. S. Eliot,

> No poet, no artist of any art, has his complete meaning alone. His significance, his appreciation is the appreciation of his relation to the dead poets and artists. You cannot value him alone; you must set him, for contrast and comparison, among the dead.[117]

This we can take as the weak sense of intertextuality, and it concentrates upon the action of the reader or critic in establishing intertextual links. More recently the American critic Harold Bloom has written extensively of 'the anxiety of influence' suffered by writers, and their attempts to escape from the stern gaze of their predecessors; here we are dealing with a stronger variant.

In cases where there is a direct and specific link between two texts the term 'transtextuality' is sometimes used, to distinguish such relatively simple examples from the more complex cases where influence and reference are extensive and diffuse. According to this usage our Inspector Clouseau example would involve transtextuality rather than intertextuality.

Even some relatively direct examples of intertextual or transtextual reference can nevertheless involve layers of complexity. To take one example; Joseph Conrad's character Marlow appears in four of his fictional works, and yet it would be dangerous to assume that Marlow is necessarily the 'same person' in each – many critics have commented that he seems rather different in *Chance* (the last work in which he appears). Again, on the first page of the second work in which Marlow appears – *Heart of Darkness* – the 'outer' narrator remarks of the five individuals (including Marlow) who are gathered together that, 'Between us there was, as I have already said somewhere, the bond of the sea.' That 'somewhere' is, most readers assume, in Conrad's short story *Youth*, in which a seemingly identical group of individuals hear Marlow's tale, and an unnamed outer narrator makes just this point concerning the bond of the sea. We are led to believe, therefore, that these two works share the same fictional space, and that the reference to *Youth* in *Heart of Darkness* is not a reference to a work of fiction, but to *Youth* as an account 'by' the unnamed narrator rather than by Joseph Conrad.

A slightly more problematic situation occurs when a writer takes a fictional character from another writer's work and uses him or her

---

[117] T. S. Eliot, 'Tradition and the Individual Talent', in *Selected Essays*, p.15.

within a new work – as Jean Rhys did with characters from Charlotte
Brontë's *Jane Eyre* in her own work *Wide Sargasso Sea*. Most readers
take it – correctly, I think – that here it is not a matter of the two sets
of characters sharing the same fictional space: there is an oppositional or revisionist element in Rhys's book which both challenges
and complements Brontë's. This is a different sort of transtextuality
from that found in Conrad's Marlow works.

A yet more complex example is to be found in the opening
paragraph of Mark Twain's *The Adventures of Huckleberry Finn*, an
opening paragraph which, we should remember, follows Twain's
humorous 'Notice' warning against attempts to find moral, motive
or plot in his narrative, and his explanation of the dialects used in
the novel.

> You don't know about me, without you have read a book by the name of
> *The Adventures of Tom Sawyer*, but that ain't no matter. That book was
> made by Mr Mark Twain, and he told the truth, mainly. There was things
> which he stretched, but mainly he told the truth.

The most obvious thing about this example is the playing with levels
of fiction and extra-fictional reference which it involves. It purports
on one level to be a comment by a character in his own right as
author on another book reported by the real-world author, which
includes the same character, but as real-world individual rather than
fictional character. But as the reader of this opening paragraph is
holding a book which the cover tells him or her is 'by Mark Twain',
the effect is to move us in and out of real-world and fictional-world
realities whilst simultaneously moving us between two interlinked
but nonetheless differing texts. And the fact that the modern reader
knows that 'Mark Twain' is a pseudonym adds to the complexity of
the passage – as does the almost cheeky statement that the earlier
book is not wholly truthful. (The latter assertion purports on one
level to be a real-world comment on another real-world report –
interpreting 'real-world' within the outer fictional frame – but it can
also be taken as Twain's own camouflaged admission that the earlier
work did not quite measure up to certain larger truth-criteria.)

We have ended up, again, with the question of truth – not altogether surprisingly as intertextual and transtextual references
always seem to threaten the fictive illusion, to expose the work of
fiction as artifice and thus to raise the issue of the force of fictional
assertions or utterances in the real world. In this view intertextuality
has much in common with fictional self-reference, another literary
technique which – like the Russian Formalists' foregrounding or
Brecht's alienation effect – exposes the conventions upon which
literary illusion or (in Coleridge's term) suspension of disbelief rest.

In spite of a long history of marked scepticism towards the truth claims of literature on the part of literary critics, there is an equally strong tradition that can be traced from writer to writer, and which insists that the aim of literary expression is that of truth. A famous letter of Keats's (to Benjamin Bailey, 22 November 1817) insistently returns to the assertion that 'What the imagination seizes as Beauty must be truth – whether it existed before or not', and William Empson, commenting upon the fact that his mother thought that his poem 'To an Old Lady' was about her mother, whereas it was actually about herself, remarks that 'It proved that the poem was true.'[118]

In reading literature readers make enormously complex manipulations of levels of meaning in works, and direct similarly complex sets of relationship between literary works and extra-literary reality. But such complexity is part of the means whereby literature can refer outside itself, can affirm, can lie, and can reveal the truth – it is not a reason to disbelieve that such reference is possible.

[118] I take the comment from a BBC radio programme on Empson, which contained an interview between Empson and Christopher Ricks.

VI
Reception

The reading of literary works, their 'affects', their influence and reception over time – these are aspects of the literary process that have come in for detailed scrutiny in recent years but which have been accorded little – or, on occasions, no – attention by critics and theorists at various times. The New Critical concentration upon the text 'itself' often involved subsuming the reader or reading in the text, so that whilst arguing vehemently against a consideration of the reader or readers, or the 'affects' of literary works, these elements of the literary process were smuggled in to the text, and what were often the critic's personal and subjective opinions and responses were displaced into 'the words on the page'. We can witness one probable reason for this sleight-of-hand in W. K. Wimsatt and Monroe Beardsley's essay, 'The Affective Fallacy': a text is *there*, accessible, seemingly unchanging, but

> The report of some readers . . . that a poem or story induces in them vivid images, intense feelings, or heightened consciousness, is not anything which can be refuted nor anything which it is possible for the objective critic to take into account.[119]

According to Wimsatt and Beardsley, the 'affective fallacy', 'begins by trying to derive the standard of criticism from the psychological effects of the poem and ends in impressionism and relativism.'[120] Whereas the literary work is public, accessible, fixed, and single, its affects or reception are private, inaccessible, and awe-inspiringly multiple – so the argument runs.

But as a number of commentators have pointed out, if this vision of inaccessibility and multiplicity is found so frightening that all consideration of a work's reception and effects are ruled out of court, the return of the repressed occurs within the text itself: in multiple interpretations and readings reliant upon private associations.

It is perhaps partly for this reason that in recent years an

[119] *The Verbal Icon*, p.32.
[120] *The Verbal Icon*, p.21.

increasing amount of interest in the topic of reception has been displayed by literary critics. But there are other reasons. The growth of Media Studies, building importantly upon sociological traditions, has been responsible for more and more sophisticated studies of mass-media audiences, and for increasing scepticism concerning purely textual studies of the mass-media. And finally, we can again draw attention to the spectre of the common reader. The more literary critics have become concerned by an apparently growing gap between ordinary readers and academic readers, the more they have been forced to pay attention to readers and reading, and to develop theories which incorporate both.

Performance

If we are to consider the reception of literature then we have to say something concerning the difference between the performance arts such as drama, and non-performance arts such as (generally speaking) the novel. Poetry developed as a performance art, and some of its characteristics can only be fully understood in the light of this fact, and at certain times prose fiction has flourished in performance – that is, through readings to audiences. But as a generalization we can venture that drama is a performance art, whereas the novel and poetry are most usually read silently by the private reader today.

What is of theoretical interest about performance is that it is undeniably *creative* rather than a merely passive transmission of the author's meanings or intentions. The actor who interprets the rôle of Hamlet is attracted by what is 'in' the play, but also by what it offers him in respect of creative possibility. In like manner it can be claimed that the theatre audience is less active, has less scope for creative imagining, than the private reader.[121] Watching a performance of *Hamlet* we cannot imagine all the possibilities that are available to us when we read the text of the play.

Now the interesting question which this raises is as follows. Are there aspects of the normal reader's response to – say – a novel which are equivalent to the creative rôle of the actor (or theatre director)? Do we 'perform' novels to ourselves, mentally? Does the silent reader combine the functions of director, actor, and theatre audience? Is this why watching a film of a book spoils our subsequent reading of the book – that it interferes with our internal performing of it? If so this has important implications, for it establishes that reading is not just the passive reception of an authorial meaning, but the creative production of something (meanings,

[121] See R. A. Sharpe, 'The Private Reader and the Listening Public', in Jeremy Hawthorn (ed.), *Criticism and Critical Theory*, London, Arnold, 1984, p.15 ff.

interpretations, appreciations, responses) from the text. And that, if true, raises many subsequent questions – as to whether or not there are valid and invalid forms of reader-creativity, for instance. And just as most directors (probably all, actually) assume that they are choosing one of a number of different possible performances of a single text, so too it might follow that a single text of a novel can be silently 'performed' by the reader in a variety of different ways. Here, perhaps, we are back with Wimsatt and Beardsley's nightmare: a single text replaced by the mirror-wilderness of readings and performances. But it may also be E. D. Hirsch's nightmare too: a single authorial meaning replaced by a multitude of creative readings.

At this stage it is necessary to admit that silent reading and the production and reception of performances cannot fully be assimilated. For a start, in performance interpretation and response are compartmentalized to a considerable extent, whereas in silent reading the two form part of a far more integrated whole. Furthermore private reading seems to involve a far greater 'carrying' of mutually exclusive possible interpretations than does (or can) performance: the director and actor are limited in the number of alternative responses to and interpretations of the play that can be maintained in a single performance, whereas the private reader is far less limited and constrained. (Although it should be added that reading is logically prior to performing: the director and the actors must read the text of the play before they work on a performance, and that initial reading may be as free-ranging as is a standard private reading.)

If we compare the theatre audience and the silent reader alone, the differences between the two are not hard to seek. Firstly, as I have said, the audience *receives an interpretation*, whereas the reader *interprets*. (The audience may interpret the interpretation it receives, but this is clearly a secondary process.) Secondly, the audience responds *collectively*, the reader *individually* (although tradition, training, convention impose collective elements on reading.) Thirdly, the audience has to experience the work *at the speed and in the sequence determined by the performance*, the reader chooses his or her *own speed and sequence*. It is true that according to convention skipping sections in a novel or peeking at the last page are frowned upon and considered illegitimate, but no-one has ever claimed that readers are not allowed to pause when they like, to re-read passages (Sterne actually instructs the reader to do this at one point in *Tristram Shandy*), or to read at his or her preferred speed. The writer (or director) thus has more power over the reception of a performed work than over that of a privately read work – although serial publication gave novelists a certain power that ordinary book publication did not. The performance arts exert their price for this control however: performances are limited by the constraints of an audience's ability to be in one particular place for a certain length of time, and by other physical constraints: a theatre audience can only be so large, for instance. It is time, however, to look at readers and readings in more detail.

Reader(s), Reading(s)

My heading is clumsy, but it does have the merit that it reminds us how less willing we are to offer generalizations about literary reception today, how talk of 'the reader' seems to pose too many questions to be accepted without unease. Most literary works have one author but many readers, and these readers can engage in more than one reading of the same work of literature. Recent critical theory has familiarized us with terms such as 'the implied reader', 'the empirical reader', and 'the ideal reader'. It has also familiarized us with titles such as *A Reading of 'Paradise Lost'*, titles which prepare us for the experience of learning about what will be presented as one of a number of such 'readings'. 'Reading' here is very close to 'interpretation', but other recent criticism has directed our attention to actual reading experiences far more, reading experiences which to a greater or a lesser extent vary from person to person.

As I have suggested, my own belief is that those mass-media researchers who demonstrated that different members of the audience of a given television programme experienced it in different, possibly radically different, ways, have had a significant effect on literary critics and theorists. No longer can the critic use the royal 'we' and feel that he or she describes what all readers of the same text experience. This change of perspective has raised a number of new theoretical questions about readers and readings, towards which I would now like to direct my attention – starting with readers.

Is there such a thing as an ideal reader? We can perhaps best tackle this by asking if there is an ideal reader for a single work – say *Hamlet*, or 'In Memoriam', or *Portnoy's Complaint* – for if the answer to this question is 'no', then clearly there can be no such thing as an ideal reader for all works. Let me take myself as a reader of *Portnoy's Complaint*. As I am neither American nor Jewish it might seem clear that I have relatively poor qualifications as a reader of this novel – not so poor as a Japanese woman or a Nigerian Muslim – but poor nonetheless. A lecturer introducing this novel to a group of British students would probably feel the need to say something about its Jewish–American context, and although I have some knowledge of this it is not extensive. On this account if we wish to find the ideal reader of *Portnoy's Complaint* then we should look for someone who already has a detailed knowledge of this context.

But here common sense starts to raise a number of objections. Is not one of the pleasures we extract from literary works precisely that of learning about a different culture, about people we might not meet in everyday life? Moreover, is it not an advantage for me to be able to compare the culture described in Philip Roth's novel – its conventions, customs, and traditions – with my own? Does not this give me the ability to extract something from this work that perhaps an American Jewish reader might lack in his or her reading?

Note that I am not saying that I am a *more* suitable reader of the novel than someone more attuned to the culture in which it is set, only that such a person and I would draw different things from our readings of the work, would have a different relationship to what is described.

All of this may seem like stating the obvious, but its implications – although well known to us in practice – are often ignored in spite of the fact that they are far from trivial. A single literary text offers a range of different reading experiences to different readers. If you are a miner, then Zola's descriptions of miners' working lives in *Germinal* will appear less shocking and disturbing than if you are a bank manager who has never been within fifty miles of a coal mine. One of the things that makes literary works valuable is that very different readers, separated by time and space, can draw different benefits, knowledge, pleasure from the same work. (And this, incidentally, is the reason why the same person, in process of continual historical change and development, can draw different things from successive readings of the same literary work; as Jonathan Culler has pointed out, 'To speak of an ideal reader is to forget that reading has a history'.)[122]

Now note that I am *not* saying that the 'meaning' of a literary work varies from person to person, nor am I saying that different readers' experiences of the same literary work will bear no relationship to one another. As I have already pointed out, there are real problems in talking of a literary work's 'meaning', and (to take my second point), literary-critical discussion often involves sharing those aspects of our literary readings that we have in common as well as considering those aspects that we do not. Criticism is one of the ways whereby personal and private elements in our response to and interpretation of literary works are made public and available to others. Moreover, the similarities in our literary responses and interpretations offer strong evidence for our having much in

[122]Culler, p.53, n.3.

common as human beings in spite of important differences and variations between us.

Norman Holland uses the analogy of our response to optical illusions to demonstrate that we are active and creative in interpreting signs, not just passively open to another's meaning.[123] But what he fails to consider is psychological evidence into the extent to which human beings do or do not share similar responses to the same optical illusion, research which demonstrates that all human beings respond in identical manner to some such illusions, whereas some are culturally specific.[124] The analogy would suggest, then, that those experiences (interpreted widely) that we have in common with others will lead us to respond to and interpret literary works in similar ways, those experiences which are personally or culturally specific will lead us to respond or interpret in more unique ways. There is certainly an element of truth in this: we communicate well with those with whom we have much in common. I think that it was King Charles II who explained the appeal of a popular preacher by remarking that, 'His nonsense suits their nonsense'. But it is also the case that our experience of daily life, of communicating with those different from ourselves, teaches us skills of sympathy and empathy, develops the imaginative ability to put ourselves in other peoples' positions. And these skills are utilized and developed in the reading of literature.

To Coleridge is due the credit for one particular phrase which has done much service in discussions of the way in which a reader may adapt his or her normal beliefs and assumptions so as better to be able to enter the world of a literary work. In *Biographia Literaria*, writing of the collaboration between himself and Wordsworth in the production of the *Lyrical Ballads*, Coleridge notes that as his contribution to the collection

> it was agreed, that my endeavours should be directed to persons and characters supernatural, or at least romantic; yet so as to transfer from our inward nature a human interest and a semblance of truth sufficient to procure for these shadows of imagination that willing suspension of disbelief for the moment, which constitutes poetic faith.

'Suspension of disbelief', then, involves the reader's disregarding or withdrawing those normal value-judgements or belief-entailments which govern his or her extra-literary responses to people, situations, opinions. But for this to take place, Coleridge recognizes, the literary work must provide the reader with a 'semblance of truth'

---

[123]Norman N. Holland, 'Re-Covering "The Purloined Letter": Reading as a Personal Transaction', in Suleiman and Crosman, p.364.
[124] See for example A. R. Luria, *Cognitive Development*, London, Harvard UP, 1976, pp.20–47.

and a 'human interest'; the reader must feel that in giving away the right to judge or respond as he or she would do in everyday life, there is some reward in terms of truth and human interest. Literary reading, in this view, is a way of exploring states of mind unavailable to us in day-to-day living, and this has been one of the traditional justifications of the reading of literature: it expands our sympathy for other people and our understanding of the world by encouraging the free (or freer) play of the imagination.

Similar arguments are associated with the view that literary works – like other art works – should be approached in a special way, that there is an 'aesthetic attitude' appropriate to works of art without which we are unable to benefit from their potential powers for imaginative renewal. Now there clearly is some truth in this. We do not normally approach the reading of literature in an instrumentalist frame of mind, wanting to *use* the work for a fixed end. (If we read a work of literature merely to be able to pass an examination or to further our academic career it can be argued that we approach it wrongly, and in a manner not designed to allow us to benefit from its specific qualities.) But this does not necessarily mean that *all* our normal values and assumptions are suspended. When an actor in a play shouts 'Fire!' we do not, it is true, run for the exit – but we do make internal reference to what such a cry signifies in the extra-theatrical world. Literary works do not induce to simple action in the way that real-world experiences do, we assume; when Virginia Woolf said of the novels written by Wells, Bennett, and Galsworthy that they left the reader with a feeling of incompleteness and dissatisfaction such that in order to complete them 'it seems necessary to do something – to join a society, or, more desperately, to write a cheque',[125] then we understand that a criticism of some force is being levelled. Nevertheless, we should not therefore assume that literary works have no relation to the beliefs and actions of the reader, only that these differ from the relations between our beliefs and actions and our dealings with people and events in the everyday world.

Moreover, as a number of more recent critics have pointed out, it is possible for a literary work to be given an 'oppositional reading' – in other words, for the reader to do the opposite of suspending his or her disbelief and, instead, bringing a hostile scrutiny to the values and assumptions of the world of the work or the implied author. Such oppositional reading almost inevitably militates against aesthetic empathy: to read in an oppositional manner one needs to be aware of the work as work, as aesthetic or fictional construct, rather

[125] 'Mr. Bennett and Mrs. Brown', p.326.

than as 'window on the world'.

Let us turn to some different ways in which reader may be categorized, ways which can help us to pinpoint some of the complex ways in which unique and common elements combine in our reading of literary works.

The intended reader is a conceptualization designed to indicate a writer's sense of the reader(s) he or she expects. In the process of writing most writers have both a general sense of potential readers' knowledge, prejudices, experience, and also more particular conceptions of individual readers. These last may be real people who the writer can envisage standing behind the writing-desk and responding to what is written, or imaginary personages who serve as vicarious readers, helping to lessen the writer's feeling of isolation or lack of confidence – or giving the writer someone to react against and argue with. (In Edinburgh, Summer 1986, the Canadian novelist Margaret Atwood reported that she had imagined a masculine figure of authority as reader while writing her early novels, but had subsequently imagined being read by a woman as she composed her later work.)

A writer will certainly be possessed, too, of a sense of the actual readers he or she will be likely to get – although an established writer with a well-defined readership will be likely to have a far more focused sense of potential readers than an unknown writer producing unconventional and revolutionary work in a very fluid social or literary context.

It is important to remember that the intended reader is often far from being the ideal reader: indeed, it may be better to talk of the 'expected' than the 'intended' reader. In *Heart of Darkness*, for example, Joseph Conrad has his 'inner' narrator Marlow offer a number of extremely derogatory and frustrated comments about the understanding of those in the small group of people listening to his narrative. It seems certain that Marlow's comments represent at least part of Conrad's own feelings about his own expected readers, and as Marlow makes clear, such readers could in no way be described as 'ideal' recipients of what Conrad was writing. The example is an interesting one because it shows how a writer may attempt to educate his own readers, to get them to consider their inadequacy as readers of a particular work and – let us hope – to do something about it. (Much of Wordsworth's Preface to his 'Lyrical Ballads' has the aim of educating his readers so that they can profitably read the poems in the collection: what Conrad does within the work itself, Wordsworth does in a separate Preface.) It is characteristic of writers who are dissatisfied either with who their readers are, or what their readers are like, that they try to make their readers more self-conscious as readers. Roy Fisher has an intriguing poem entitled 'One World', first published in the journal *Stand*, about a class of poor children the poet taught in Birmingham. The poem ends as follows:

> About them
> I know I can generalize without offence.
> But to name names: if John Snook,
> Anne Pouney or Brian Davidson,
> Pat Aston or Royston Williams,
> should, of their own accord and unprompted,
> read over this and remember me –
> if they're offended, they can tell me about it:
> it would be good to know
> we all look at the same magazines.[126]

The effect of this naming of (we presume) real people who will never know that they have been so named is to make the actual readers of Fisher's poem poignantly aware of the fact that they constitute a limited group, and to be self-conscious about this.

Talk of the intended reader should not obscure the fact that writers often (perhaps usually) have a very sophisticated and complex view of their potential readership or audience. It is clear that both Shakespeare and Dickens were fully aware of the stratified and varied nature of those for whom they were writing, and since the advent of writing the poet has been aware that he or she may be composing for posterity. Conrad talks of the unexpected readers that a writer may have in his novel *Under Western Eyes*. It is difficult to read John Donne's poem 'The Relique', in which the poet writes of his grave being opened at some future time and of the wonderful interpretations of the significance of the 'bracelet of bright haire about the bone' that will then be made, without seeing it as in part a displacement of Donne's imagining his poem being read in future ages by those without personal acquaintance with him or his mistress.

A term cognate to that of the intended reader is *the inscribed reader* – that is, the reader actually indicated within the text as suitable or expected for the text. A writer commonly referred to in this context is Jane Austen: her narrators characteristically appear to make certain assumptions about the readers an Austen novel will have, such that from the texts of the novels themselves we can read off information about the reader expected – one sharing particular social and moral assumptions, and possessed of sensitivity to the

---

[126] Roy Fisher, 'One World', *Stand* 12(1), 1972, p.4.

nuances of human behaviour and of interpretative skills applicable both to language and to actions. As we read a novel such as *Pride and Prejudice* we are – whatever our personal characteristics, whatever society or culture we belong to – encouraged to become more and more like the inscribed reader contained in the work.

In recent years investigation into *empirical readers* has gathered considerable momentum, although it has only scratched the surface of what is potentially accomplishable. Such research can involve categorizing the readers of different literary works according to gender, age, social class, or whatever – and by extending such analysis to cover historical changes it can map the changes and consistencies in a particular work's readership. But it can also focus on what we may term the *mechanics of reading*: where do most readers pause in their reading? How long do they take to read a given work? Under what circumstances do they skip or reread? When do they read more slowly or more quickly? When and where do they read? How does their reading mesh in with other activities? Such research is very difficult to conduct without disturbing that which it investigates, and there is no doubt that it is at a very early stage of development today. Researchers have placed electronic devices on the eyeball and have thus been able to plot viewers' eye-movements as they study paintings, but comparable research into readers' reading habits hardly exist.

Let us turn to *readings*. Here certain key questions need attention. To what extent is the reader (or should he or she be) active or passive in reading? In what ways does reading involve creation as well as 'reception'? How similar are different readings of the same work – and how similar can or should they be? A good starting point to the consideration of such questions is Keats's poem 'On Sitting Down to Read *King Lear* Once again'.

O golden tongued Romance, with serene lute!
    Fair plumed Syren, Queen of far-away!
    Leave melodizing on this wintry day,
Shut up thine olden pages, and be mute:
Adieu! for, once again, the fierce dispute
    Betwixt damnation and impassion'd clay
    Must I burn through; once more humbly assay
The bitter-sweet of this Shakespearian fruit:
Chief Poet! and ye clouds of Albion,
    Begetters of our deep eternal theme!
When through the old oak Forest I am gone,
    Let me not wander in a barren dream,
But, when I am consumed in the fire
Give me new Phoenix wings to fly at my desire.

Note first of all how important the reader's *predisposition* is here seen to be. Keats is of course concerned with rereading here, but predisposition is a crucial aspect of any reading (although it is probably more subject to modification with initial readings). Secondly, witness how the poem zig-zags between words and phrases suggesting reader passivity ('humbly assay', 'consume') and those suggesting reader activity ('burn through', 'fly'). It is this view of the reading process as both active and passive that makes Keats's poem so interesting. For Keats the work is neither created by the reader nor passively to be received by him or her: reading involves interaction between the work and the reader. A range of theorists have, in recent years, led us to see the reading process in a far more polarized way: either as the irresponsible reader's 'playing with texts', or as the writer-patriarch's imposing a meaning on the reader. But literature offers both the possibility of imaginative creativity and freedom and also a discipline.

Not surprisingly, such polarized views have led to the equally polarized assertions that either all readings of the same work should (ideally) be identical, or that every reading is totally unique: either the reader as slave, or the reader as absolute monarch. Both positions lead to insuperable problems. If all readings should, ideally, be the same, then *Hamlet* must be a rather inadequate work to have provoked such a variety of responses and interpretations. And if all readings should be unique then how can we discuss literary works at all? If the reader has absolute power, then why not keep rereading the same work indefinitely? Why label some works as better than others? (In like manner – if all readings should ideally be the same, then what is the point of rereading works?). An interactive view of reading frees us from such sterile polarities and recognizes the necessary mixture of the unique and the shared, the personal and the social in reading and response.

A theory of reading must also recognize that we experience literary works over time, and that this applies not just to the period of time when we are actually reading, but also to the after-life literary works have in our consciousnesses. This is why there has been debate about whether a literary work is 'object' or 'process', a debate that will end only when we recognize that it is in a sense both – that to repeat Douglas Hewitt's words, it is both 'a created object to which we look back and an experience which we undergo'. Criticism needs to pay attention to both aspects of the reader–work relationship, and to variations in the way in which different readers undergo the experience of reading.

Where does this leave the notion of correctness or legitimacy? Can we still say that a particular reading is *wrong*? Well, to start with, we can often demonstrate that a critical interpretation is based on a misreading – the syntax of a sentence misunderstood, a word misinterpreted, and so on. We can also indicate that a reading is at odds with what an author intended (back to intention!) – but this may not mean that it is unproblematically wrong. I have always disliked Philip Larkin's poem 'The Whitsun Weddings' because it has always seemed to me to offer a patronizing view of working-class people. In an interview with John Haffenden Larkin has made it clear that he did not feel superior or patronizing at all, that he thought it 'wonderful' to be in touch with 'the young lives starting up'.[127] Nonetheless, I find it impossible to read the poem without feeling that the people described are viewed as without significant individuality, and such a view I still find patronizing. We are here in the realm not so much of 'reading', but more of interpretation and evaluation. It is not a question as whether I have or have not misunderstood the poem – or Larkin's intentions – but of how I interpret or evaluate his view of working-class people as presented in the poem. Now my interpretation or evaluation may still be wrong, but it is in no way founded upon a misreading if it is.

But some readings are wrong. Even that most passionate advocate of the individual reader's freedom to read and respond according to his or her own psychological makeup – Norman Holland – agrees that there must be some limits set to what can legitimately be done with a literary work. Holland is, it must be said, somewhat inconsistent about this matter in his *5 Readers Reading* (Yale UP, 1975). On page 13 of his book he writes:

> To be sure, professional critics often write as though they were establishing a 'correct' reading, but the fact is that critics themselves disagree more than they agree. [*A dubious assertion, in my view* – JH] Evidently, therefore, one cannot posit even for highly trained readers a 'correct' response in any given reader's mind to something definitively 'in' the text.

But on page 219 we are told

> Yet the words can't be just anything. Miss Emily, [in Faulkner's *A Rose for Emily*] we have noted, cannot be an Eskimo – at least not without doing violence to the text.

The contradiction seems inescapable.

However, if we accept what a number of theorists have argued – that literary works are by definition *suggestive* rather than prescriptive, naturally productive of a range of differing responses in the minds of different readers – then certain aspects of the mental responses to literary works that we enjoy are improperly labelled

[127] John Haffenden, *Viewpoints*, London, Faber, 1981, p.125.

either correct or incorrect. If, in reading Ezra Pound's poem 'In a Station of the Metro', I have a mental image of pink petals and another reader has a mental image of white ones, that does not mean to say that either of us is necessarily wrong, any more than one of two different performances of the same play is necessarily wrong. R. A. Sharpe has argued that 'interpretations are under-determined by the work'[128] – in some ways making much the same point as it made by those critics who see literary or artistic works as 'suggestive'. If true, this entails a recognition of the non-illegitimacy of (some or all) rival or contradictory interpretations of the same work.

Some literary works are more suggestive than others, more open-ended and less constraining with regard to readers' interpretations or responses. A poet possessed of Keats's 'negative capability' is likely to write poems which allow for a greater variety of reading experiences than, say, poems by the older Wordsworth.

Reading/Rereading

With certain literary works we have perhaps the only examples of writing that, the more familiar we are with them the more we nevertheless want to read them again. Our desire to reread literary works is surely linked to that quality of suggestiveness or interpreta-tive underdetermination of which I have just spoken. Although the reader is much freer to entertain multiple and even contradictory responses and interpretation to a work than is a member of a theatre audience, even this greater freedom has its limits, and rereading allows for the experiencing of new responses, new imaginative experiences, and the consideration of new interpretations of a given work.

Moreover, if a reader's predispositions have a conditioning effect upon a reading, then the rereading of a literary work (for which one's expectations and predispositions must differ from those which preceded the initial reading) must be different from a first reading. With a novel, for example, when we know 'what will happen' then we may lose tension, curiosity, the imaginative testing out of varied hypotheses, but we probably gain a greater sense of the novel's structure and interrelations. If a first reading allows us to derive maximum experience of the novel as process, a subsequent reading will allow us to increase our appreciation of the novel as object, as crafted whole. Furthermore, the reader will have changed between first and second reading of a work (if for no other reason

---

[128] Sharpe, *Contemporary Aesthetics*, p.120.

than that the first reading will have altered him or her), and so if reading involves interaction between the reader and the work then the interactive process will be different the second time around. As Margaret Atwood expresses it bluntly

> Reading is also a process and it changes you. You aren't the same person after you've read a particular book as you were before, and you will read the next book, unless both are Harlequin Romances, in a slightly different way. When you read a book, it matters how old you are and when you read it and whether you are male or female, or from Canada or India. There is no such thing as a truly universal literature, partly because there are no truly universal readers.[129]

Society

To talk of literary reception as if it could be divided neatly between 'the reader' and 'society' is clearly open to certain objections. Societies are made up of individuals, and individuals are produced within specific societies. Nevertheless it can be fruitful to look at the issue of literary reception through a wide-angle lens, to consider how a single work is 'received' in different societies at the same time, or in the same society over a period of time. *Reception theory* is the term often given to such a project, and it is particularly associated with Swiss and West-German theoreticians who have studied the larger patterns of literary preference or interpretation. In a very influential essay the German theorist Hans Robert Jauss has argued that a reader's 'horizon of expectations' both determines and is altered by the reading of a particular work. Jauss singles out three ways in which a writer can anticipate a reader's response, and these seem to represent what he sees as the three main determinants of the reader's 'horizon of expectations'.

> first, by the familiar standards or the inherent poetry of the genre; second, by the implicit relationships to familiar works of the literary-historical context; and third, by the contrast between fiction and reality . . . The third factor includes the possibility that the reader of a new work has to perceive it not only within the narrow horizon of his literary expectations but also within the wider horizon of his experience of life.[130]

It will be seen that Jauss's emphasis is more literary than social: 'experience of life' comes a poor third in the above list, and later on in his essay he argues that an 'unknown' work is best understood 'if the text is considered in contrast to the background of the works which the author could expect his contemporary public to know

---

[129] Margaret Atwood, *Second Words*, Toronto, House of Anansi Press, 1982, p.345.
[130] Hans Robert Jauss, 'Literary History as a Challenge to Literary Theory', in *New Directions in Literary History*, p.18.

either explicitly or implicitly.'[131]

My own feeling is that such literary influences are nearly always subordinate to the reader's 'experience of life', and have to be seen in relation to them. There are no purely literary reasons why the eighteenth century preferred *King Lear* with a happy ending, or why Donne's reputation was comparatively low in the nineteenth century and very much higher in the twentieth, or why Flaubert's *Madame Bovary* and D. H. Lawrence's *The Rainbow* should have been subject to legal prosecution when first published while they are now accepted on school reading syllabuses with hardly the bat of an eyelid. As T. S. Eliot has commented, each age demands different things from poetry, and our literary criticism too will reflect the things that the age demands. Such matters are not internal to literature: the bitter disputes which raged around Wordsworth's early poetry on its first publication cannot be understood independently of sudden and powerful social and political changes, major political and ideological pressures, in the Europe of the late eighteenth century. At any given time we may be more conscious of our disagreements than about what we have in common; the virtue of historical and social study of literary reception is that it reveals the pressures and movements to which we may be unconsciously subject in our literary preferences, responses, and interpretations.

The recent development of the women's movement offers us a useful illustration of the extremely complex interlinking of socio-historical and political forces on the one hand, and literary appreciation on the other. The roots of the resurgence of an autonomous women's movement in the late 1960s and early 1970s in USA and Western Europe are complex, but it seems likely that in addition to objective social factors such as the politicization of young people attendant upon the Vietnam war, expanded higher-education opportunities for women alongside continued material and ideological discrimination against women in public and private life, the influence of both older and more recent literary works by women was important. But if literary works contributed to the contemporary growth of the women's movement, this movement has had an enormous effect on the writing and reading of literature. Older works have been rediscovered, reread, reinterpreted, and revalued; substantial encouragement and guidance has been provided for new women writers (and male ones too), and what can fairly be termed a new readership has been created. Socio-historical and literary influences have a dialectical relationship so far as the creation and alteration of literary audiences are concerned, and the

[131] Jauss, p.23.

respective importance of the socio-historical and the literary may rise or fall at different periods. Nonetheless, my own view is that the latter is subordinate to the former, even though this may not always be apparent. My disquiet about reception theory is that too often it concentrates upon how literature is received by society while ignoring how society is received by literature – and the connotations of 'reception' are perhaps too much of passivity and a one-way process.

Effect

According to W. H. Auden, 'Poetry makes nothing happen.'[132] According to T. S. Eliot, 'The fiction that we read affects our behaviour towards our fellow men, affects our patterns of ourselves.'[133] The critic Stein Haugom Olsen has accepted that literature may change a reader's beliefs 'as a side-effect', and may thus affect his or her actions, but he argues that 'it seems unlikely that a work can influence action through its literary qualities.'[134]

Governments and powerful authorities have, however, consistently displayed great concern with what literature is published and what is not published: on the one hand censorship and repression of writers, on the other subsidies to writers, Poets Laureate, the establishment of literary works and their study within the educational system. Some people not known for their cultural or artistic delusions of grandeur clearly believe that literature does make things happen. Is it possible that it does so only as a side-effect, rather than as literature? My problem with this argument is that of its circularity: literature is defined in terms of its aesthetic properties, aesthetic properties are seen necessarily to involve no tendency to cause action, and so if people's behaviour is changed through the reading of a literary work then this must have been a side-effect rather than a genuinely literary effect.

Now it is certainly possible to argue that the way in which literature is taught and studied in schools and universities in Britain and America very often *encourages* readers to consider literary works as means to contemplation rather than action. B. Cameron, in an interesting article entitled 'Language and the Alteration of Human Behaviour', relates this to the view that literary works do not refer to the real world, do not make statements about extra-literary reality.

---

[132]W. H. Auden, 'In Memory of W. B. Yeats', in Edward Mendelson (ed.), *The English Auden*, London, Faber, 1977, p.242.
[133] T. S. Eliot, 'Religion and Literature', in *Selected Essays*, p.393.
[134] Olsen, p.206.

> By very few teachers is poetry treated as news, however old, about the
> world . . . [W]ho can say with certainty whether the spectatorial and
> univolved manner in which the student is led past the great human
> conflicts portrayed in art, does not contribute toward a spectatorial and
> uninvolved attitude toward what should concern him in the rest of the
> world?[135]

It is certainly the case that academics and critics rather than authors
or 'common readers' tend to believe that literature neither refers to
the world nor makes anything happen in it. Auden might appear to
be an exception, but his view that poetry makes nothing happen
coincided with his having removed himself from active political
struggle through his emigration to the United States, and others
have testified to the extreme potency of his earlier political poetry,
its ability to make plenty of things happen.[136]

Now this is not to argue that literature characteristically makes
things happen in a direct, obvious, and simple manner. Clearly the
effects of literature can range from the direct to the indirect and
highly mediated, the immediate and the very long-term. If literature
does, as Eliot argues, affect our patterns of ourselves, then its effects
may be very diffuse, indirect, inaccessible to simple measurement.
We should not talk of literary effects as if they were all on a level with
Uncle Tom's Cabin and its influence on the campaign to abolish
slavery in the United States. We have only to read the accounts by
young men and women of the effect that the publication of Wordsworth's 'Lyrical Ballads' had on them to realize that literary works
can change individuals in far more concealed and subtle manners.
To enlarge our imaginative capacities and experiences is to alter our
capacity to understand and to act in the world.

Take, as an illustration, the reader of George Eliot's novel
Middlemarch, who is forced constantly to contrast the characters'
own assessment of their position – of the economic, social, psychological and moral forces which bring pressure to bear on them – with
alternative assessments emanating from other characters or from
the narrator (or arrived at by the reader's own powers of deduction).
Any attentive reader of this novel will be forced to recognize that
while all the characters are subject to the forces and pressures I have
sketched out, some are able to recognize these forces and to learn
how to modify and even vanquish them, while other characters are

---

[135] B. Cameron, 'Language and the Alteration of Human Behaviour', *Agenda*
12(4)/13(1), Winter–Spring 1975, pp.71–2. Another article which makes a similar case
from a rather different perspective is Tony Davies, 'Education, Ideology and Literature', *Red Letters* 7, 1978, pp.4–15.
[136] See for example Arnold Kettle, 'W. H. Auden: Poetry and Politics in the Thirties',
in Jon Clark *et al.* (eds), *Culture and Crisis in Britain in the Thirties*, London, Lawrence &
Wishart, 1979, p.99.

enslaved by comparable pressures and influences. How could a reader who has recognized this not be drawn to analyse his or her own life and behaviour in the light of this reading? Well, the answer is that the reader who has been taught that literature has nothing to do with life might fail to see any connection between *Middlemarch* and his or her own life-situation. I remember being told by a white South African in the 1960s that he had studied Brecht while at university in South Africa. When I expressed surprise that this had been tolerated he explained: 'We studied it as literature, of course.' In other words, Brecht (of all writers!) had been studied as if his work said nothing about the world – and not surprisingly this study had little effect on the way most (but not all) of the students concerned saw themselves and their own lives.

None of this should be taken to suggest that the effects of literary works cannot but be good, or that readers who fail to recognize that literature refers to the world in what are often indirect and complex ways cannot respond to literary works in ways properly described as illegitimate. *Don Quixote* and *Lord Jim* both portray classic examples of such a misuse of literature, a misunderstanding of its artistic and aesthetic qualities.

Anyone who has watched a small child playing with a toy will know that human beings characteristically explore and gain mastery over their surroundings through imaginative strategies which are exceedingly complex, and which have very complicated relationships with actual (rather than imaginative) behaviour. But however indirectly, such imaginative strategies do 'make things happen', and of all the ways open to us imaginatively to explore our social, cultural, and emotional world, literature is the most sophisticated.

VII

Evaluation

According to René Wellek we cannot comprehend and analyse any work of art without reference to values,[137] and although there have been some who have argued that non-evaluative criticism is possible, it is hard to conceive of a purely descriptive criticism which has no judgemental implications, which makes no implicit or explicit reference to any scheme of values – unless we include purely formal analyses or plot synopses, which on their own hardly merit the description 'Criticism'.

Everyone, from the common reader to the most scholarly of critics, engages in literary evaluation. It is, therefore, perhaps surprising that the issue of literary evaluation should raise so many problems. Let us consider a few of them.

Firstly – what is it that we are evaluating? The obvious answer to this question would appear to be, 'the literary work'. But one of the consistent arguments in this book has been that we cannot treat the literary work as a thing-in-itself; we must examine it in the context of the dynamic relations which together form the literary process. E. D. Hirsch has commented that literary value 'must reside in the relationships between a work and its readers'; I would include other relationships, but agree that value is a relational rather than an intrinsic matter.

Does this mean, then, that any valuation of a literary work has a relative force only, is valid only with reference to a particular concatenation of circumstances? In general my answer to this question would be, 'yes', but with two important qualifications. Firstly, that the reader is the product rather than the slave of his or her age, and is thus able mentally to enter into the situation of writers and readers in other times and places – indeed, this ability is one that is fostered by the reading of literature. Thus a work that in one age has enabled readers to penetrate through to truths about themselves and their time can always have something to offer to subsequent periods. 'Our' *Hamlet* can never be quite the same as the *Hamlet* of

[137] Quoted by E. D. Hirsch in *The Aims of Interpretation*, London, U. of Chicago Press, repr. 1978, p.97.

Shakespeare's contemporaries – as I have argued, the play will never be quite the same to us twice – but nonetheless 'our' *Hamlet* contains elements of what the play was to those who witnessed its first production.

My second point is that although I believe that there is no such thing as a fixed human nature, that human beings change with the societies and cultures which form and produce them, nevertheless certain human experiences change in detail but are constant in general terms. Poverty, war, love, class-struggle – from age to age these survive, admittedly in different forms, yet sharing something of what they were in previous ages.

Traditionally, the highest value is placed on works which have been most consistently admired from age to age. Behind this attitude is the assumption that as the most fundamental and least trivial aspects of human existence are those which change most slowly, therefore a work long-admired is a work which avoids surface aspects of existence and tackles more fundamental and major questions. There is also the argument that the greatest art reaches beneath the delusory appearance of life and concerns itself with more universal laws, more abstract truths – even if these are then incorporated in depictions of the world which are rich in detail and particularity. This, it has been suggested, is the reason why major literary works are underdetermined interpretatively – they provide readers with profound truths which can be fleshed out in different ways, the implications of which can be explored in a variety of manners. Profundity has traditionally been seen as an essential attribute of major literature; if a work is profound we assume that the writing of it has involved analysis and insight as much as description and recognition.

We can call such a view a representational theory of literary value; those who hold it (we could cite Samuel Johnson and Georg Lukács) value literature by reference to the profundity and correctness of its analysis and depiction of the world. Others have approached the issue of evaluation rather differently: in terms of its *effect*, with reference to the *pleasure* it brings about, or in terms of specific *aesthetic qualities*. (It should be obvious, incidentally, that these alternatives are not necessarily mutually exclusive, but can be argued to be different aspects of the same thing.) We can also value a literary work in terms of its fulfilment of generic requirements, in terms of its realization of its author's intentions or of the inner logic of its own composition.

Practising literary critics tend – consciously or unconsciously – to adopt an attitude towards the evaluation of literary works which is either monist or pluralist. In other words, they assume either that all works can be assessed according to one set of criteria, or they believe that there are different ways in which literary works can be judged. Evaluative pluralists may believe either that each work (or each genre) has to be judged in its own, appropriate terms, or that any given work can be assessed in a variety of different ways. For evaluative monists it should theoretically be possible to *rank* all literary works on a single scale, a single league-table of worth. A critic whose evaluative comments suggest such an attitude is F. R. Leavis – although to my knowledge he never states this overtly. Leavis's criticism is dominated by an evaluative imperative: not only does it contain little descriptive discussion that is unlinked to overt evaluative judgements, but there is a constant return to the task of 'placing' them. For Leavis to 'place' a work means a number of things, but it includes an evaluative ranking of it *vis-à-vis* other works. It is likely that Helen Gardner had Leavis in mind when she protested that to 'attempt to rank writers in a literary hierarchy ignores the obvious fact that certain writers and certain works mean more to some ages and to some persons than to others, and that our responses vary very greatly with our circumstances and our age.'[138]

Evaluative monists often see evaluation in *essentialist* rather than in *relational* terms – that is, they see value residing 'in' the literary work rather than in its relationships with that which is outside it. In his book *The Theory of Literary Criticism* John Ellis provides a useful version of a relational theory of value, one which he terms *performative*. According to him, evaluations do not refer directly to properties of texts, but to their performance as literary texts. Ellis suggests an analogy with the concept of the 'great king', and notes that conceptual analysis gets us no further than that great kings 'are kings fulfilling well the function of kings.' Furthermore,

> The greatness of a king depends on the single fact of his being important and outstanding in the sequence of kings in a country. That is the sole *reason* for his categorization as a great king. But the *causes* of that categorization in his person and deeds may be many and various; so various that some of those causes may in fact exclude the others . . . Again, there is no one criterion of greatness . . .[139]

Ellis's argument is a good example of a theory of literary evaluation that is non-essentialist, pluralist, and contextual (or relational). What is important about the general lines of his argument (which I personally am in agreement with) is that they free us from the obligation to fix criteria of literary greatness or value which are located in specific *textual* properties.

---

[138] Helen Gardner, *The Business of Criticism*, London, OUP, repr. 1966, p.7.
[139] John M. Ellis, *The Theory of Literary Criticism*, London, U. of California Press, 1974, p.95.

The implications of such a shift of emphasis are explored in the following comment of Monroe Beardsley's:

> How could anything have value except in relation, direct or indirect, to the needs and desires of human beings? . . . If value is not a quality of perceptual objects, like their redness or grandeur, then it must be a relation, and consist in someone's taking a certain attitude towards the object.[140]

If, then, our 'needs and desires' change then it would follow that our valuation of literary works will also change. How do we square this with my previous comment that the highest value has, traditionally, been placed on those works which have been most consistently admired from age to age? One possible response to this question is to counter that our needs and desires change in detail – in particulars – but that there are (as I have suggested) constants in the human situation which alter in surface particulars but not in substance. The need to avoid war, to ensure that all are fed, housed and clothed adequately, the search for a situation in which human potentialities can be explored and fulfilled to the utmost – these remain constant imperatives.

Much earlier in this book I argued that 'literature' was not a stable or self-evident concept: modes of literary production, distribution and consumption change, what we now generalize about as literature has performed different *sorts* of function in the societies from which it has emerged and by which it has been reappreciated. People have read literature in a variety of different contexts for varying reasons. Some forms of evaluation will be context-specific, some will be less so. But any work which has enabled readers to understand their world and their own situation within that world better will have something to offer future readers in different times and places, for there are constancies in the laws that govern the world, there are continuities in human life and experience.

Margaret Atwood has given her view of the value of literature as follows:

> I believe that poetry is the heart of the language, the activity through which language is renewed and kept alive. I believe that fiction writing is the guardian of the moral and ethical sense of the community . . .
> [F]iction is one of the few forms left through which we may examine our society not in its particular but in its typical aspects; through which we can see ourselves and the ways in which we behave towards each other, through which we can see others and judge them and ourselves.[141]

---

[140] Beardsley, p.513.
[141] Atwood, p.346.

Atwood's emphasis – as one would expect from a practising writer –
is on the value of contemporary writing for the society for which it
springs. But, as Ezra Pound has stated, poetry is 'news that STAYS
news';[142] literary works retain a value for societies other than those
in which they were produced – a fact that puzzled (among others)
Karl Marx. Literary works retain their value for a number of reasons.
In them readers can discover their own history, can find out how
human beings became as they are. They can also reveal human
potentialities which may have been forgotten, potentialities which
do not go out of date. And in older works of literature which penetrate into underlying truths of their time readers can perceive forces
and regularities still active in later stages of history.

Feminist critics have played a particularly important function in
raising certain questions about literary evaluation in recent years.
They have pointed out that social and cultural value-judgements
enter into literary valuations, often (perhaps especially) when the
reader or critic concerned is least aware of this fact. They have
reminded us of the continuing relevance and theoretical importance
of Virginia Woolf's words:

> This is an important book, the critic assumes, because it deals with war.
> This is an insignificant book because it deals with the feelings of women
> in a drawing room.[143]

Feminist critics have forced us to recognize that evaluation too is an
interactive process, and that it involves the reader or critic's setting
his or her values against those of an author or of a text. Feminists
have also reminded us that literary works can be used in different
ways – to help us to understand our past, to give readers confidence
in their own values and to authenticate their perceptions of their
own experiences, to 'raise consciousness', to explore the nature and
reproduction of gender identities, and so on. As such, feminist
criticism has implicitly or explicitly queried the assumption that
there is such a thing as *an* aesthetic approach to a literary work. The
'constancies' in human experience of which I have spoken, then,
should not lead us to look for 'eternal values' in literary works, for
literary works will always be being read in new ways, valued for
different things, as social and cultural changes express constant
laws in varying manners. Women rather than men have babies: that
is a constant truth about the human race. But the manner in which
this fact is culturally organized and perceived changes and
develops. This is why a final evaluation of a literary work can never
be arrived at. Shakespeare's writing may be for all time, but

---

[142] In *The ABC of Reading*.
[143] Virginia Woolf, *A Room of One's Own*, London, Hogarth Press, repr. 1967, p.111.

evaluations of its importance are not. In this paradox we can see the mixture of constant and changing elements that is at the core of the literary process, at the heart of the value of literature.

Guide to Further Reading

The following notes suggest further reading in the area of literary theory, broadly defined, and not in that of literary criticism. For those interested in the latter topic, Richard Dutton's *An Introduction to Literary Criticism* (Harlow, Longman, 1984) is a useful short introduction, with its own helpful 'Suggestions for Further Reading' for those interested in deeper study.

René Wellek and Austin Warren, *Theory of Literature* first published in 1949 and subsequently published in various revised editions is still an excellent introductory study, although in certain ways it is now rather dated and obviously 'New Critical' in emphasis. It is available in a Penguin paperback edition. Much more up-to-date is Ann Jefferson and David Robey (eds), *Modern Literary Theory*. The second edition (London, Batsford, 1986), includes two extra chapters on 'Reading and Interpretation' and 'Feminist Literary Criticism' to supplement other chapters on Structuralism and Post-structuralism, Russian Formalism, New Criticism, Modern Linguistics and Literary Criticism, Psychoanalytic, and Marxist approaches. This is an ideal approach to modern schools of modern literary theory. Raman Selden's *A Reader's Guide to Modern Literary Theory* (Brighton, Harvester, 1985) is shorter and more compressed, but very readable. The latest edition of M. H. Abrams's *A Glossary of Literary Terms* (London, Holt, Rinehart & Winston, 1986) is often very useful in offering incisive comment on particular critical terms, problems, and groupings. Christopher Butler and Alastair Fowler (eds), *Topics in Criticism* (London, Longman, 1971) is a useful collection of very short extracts ordered in sections each of which is concerned with a particular set of theoretical problems. It constitutes a very useful source-book, as well as a good introduction to a range of critical issues.

In addition, the following more specialist studies can be recommended.

Interpretation and Meaning

E. D. Hirsch, Jr., *Validity in Interpretation* (London, Yale UP, 1967), &

The Aims of Interpretation (London, U. of Chicago Press, 1976).
P. D. Juhl, *Interpretation* (Princeton UP, 1980).
William Ray, *Literary Meaning* (Oxford, Blackwell, 1984).

Marxist and Socio-Historical Studies

Terry Eagleton, *Marxism and Literary Criticism* (London, Methuen, 1976); *Literary Theory: An Introduction* (Oxford, Blackwell, 1983); *The Function of Criticism* (London, Verso, 1984). The first is an excellent introduction, the second more discursive and allusive, and the third a splendid historical account of literary criticism, touching on many theoretical issues.

Robert Weimann, *Structure and Society in Literary History* (London, Lawrence & Wishart, 1977 – paperback ed. with new introduction available in USA from Johns Hopkins UP). More traditional Marxism, but excellent essays on Structuralism, narrative theory, and other topics.

Intention

David Newton-de Molina (ed.), *On Literary Intention* (Edinburgh UP, 1976). Excellent collection of key essays.

W. J. T. Mitchell (ed.), *Against Theory* (London, U. of Chicago Press, 1985). Contributions on a range of issues from the journal *Critical Inquiry*, including many concerned with problems of intention.

Structuralism and Post-Structuralism

Jonathan Culler, *Structuralist Poetics* (London, RKP, 1975), & *On Deconstruction* (London, RKP, 1983). Useful both as accounts and critiques.

Christopher Norris, *Deconstruction: Theory and Practice* (London, Methuen, 1982).

Josué V. Harari (ed.), *Textual Strategies* (Ithaca, Cornell UP, 1979; available in Britain in a Methuen paperback).

Robert Young (ed.), *Untying the Text* (London, RKP, 1981). The Harari and Young collections both contain material essential for those wishing to study the issues raised by structuralist and post-structuralist theorists.

Sociology of Literature

Jane Routh and Janet Wolff (eds), *The Sociology of Literature: Theoretical Approaches* (Keele, Sociological Review Monograph 25, 1977)

Diana Laurenson (ed.), *The Sociology of Literature: Applied Studies* (Keele, Sociological Review Monograph 26, 1978).

Feminist Theory

Josephine Donovan (ed.), *Feminist Literary Criticism* (Lexington, UP of Kentucky, 1975). A splendid introductory collection of essays.
Toril Moi, *Sexual/Textual Politics* (London, Methuen, 1985). Clear and well-argued, responding to recent theoretical problems and debates.

Reader Theory

Susan R. Suleiman and Inge Crosman (eds), *The Reader in the Text* (Princeton UP, 1980). Probably the best of a number of available anthologies/collections, with an excellent long introductory essay.
Elizabeth Freund, *The Return of the Reader* (London, Methuen, 1986). Comprehensive introductory account.

Two general works worth recommending are Stein Haugom Olsen, *The Structure of Literary Understanding* (London, CUP, 1978), and Frank Lentricchia, *After the New Criticism* (London, Athlone, 1980). Both include thought-provoking critiques of recent theoretical movements. The latter is available in Britain in a Methuen paperback.
Jeremy Hawthorn (ed.), *Criticism and Critical Theory* (London, Arnold, 1984) also contains a range of relevant articles, including one on Media Studies which raises some old problems in a fresh context.
The journals *New Literary History*, *Critical Inquiry*, and *Diacritics* regularly contain literary-theoretical articles of importance. The last-named is somewhat post-structuralist in inclination. Relevant articles can also be found in *British Journal of Aesthetics* and also the *Journal of Aesthetics and Art Criticism*. Many other literary journals also regularly publish important theoretical contributions.

Index

Literary works referred to are indexed under their respective authors.